Amy, age 9. A class exercise in design, worked from the center out. (See Daniel's stitchery exercise, worked from the outside in, page 172.) (Ivanhoe School, Bellevue, Washington.)

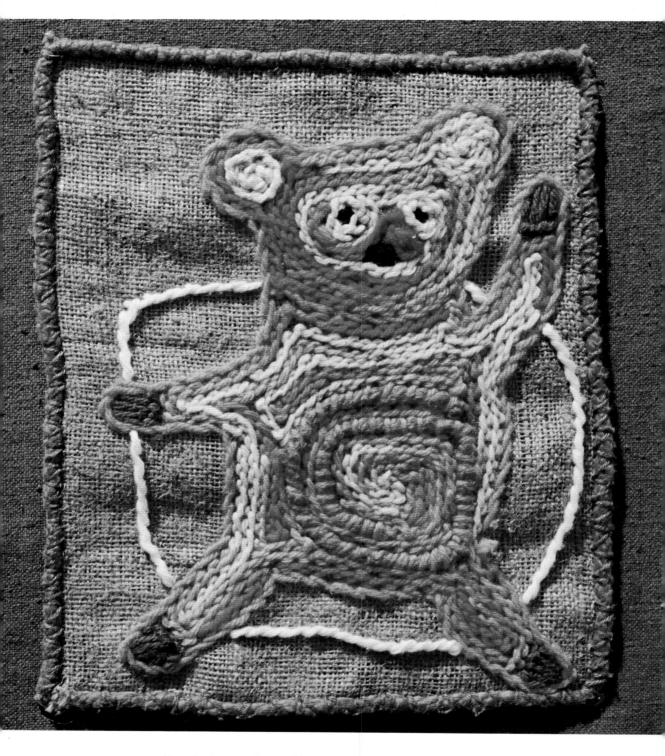

Frontispiece. Carla's Teddy Bear. Detailed description on page 45.

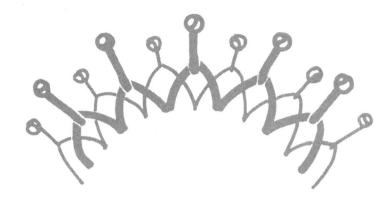

STITCHERY
FOR CHILDREN

A Manual for Teachers, Parents, and Children

Jacqueline Enthoven

VAN NOSTRAND REINHOLD COMPANY
New York   Cincinnati   Toronto   London   Melbourne

Acknowledgements

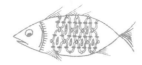

I am very grateful and deeply indebted:

To the many children whose work inspired this book — not only those whose work is pictured here, but also those whose stitcheries were just as interesting but could not be included for lack of space.

To their teachers whose enthusiasm sustained me.

To Lucille Studebaker, Coordinator of Art for the Bellevue Public Schools, Washington, for her most generous help and for going over parts of my manuscript, especially the section on Children with Special Needs.

To Arnetta Miller, head of the Northwest Center for Retarded, for her understanding and cooperation.

To Colonel and Mrs. Martin D. McAllister for their help and support. To them I owe many exciting discoveries and beautiful photographs.

To Elva Holland for her unselfish help and for the experiments she kindly conducted for me, which made much of my work possible.

To Sister Joanne Mary, head of the Art Department of Holy Names Academy in Seattle, Washington, for her beautiful lettering of my diagrams and her suggestions for the chapter on Designing Stitcheries.

To Myron Hall III, whose remarkable talents as a book designer are once again displayed in this book.

To Margaret Holton, my wise and understanding editor.

To Rosemary Enthoven, for her many valuable suggestions.

To Richard, my patient husband, without whose encouragement my books would never get written.

And last but not least, to three eager little guinea pigs, Eleanor, Richard II, and Andrew, who so happily and unsuspectingly tried out many of my ideas.

Also by Jacqueline Enthoven:
The Stitches of Creative Embroidery

Copyright © 1968 by Jacqueline Enthoven
Library of Congress Catalog Card Number 67-24702

Designed by Myron Hall III. Stitch diagrams by the author. Photographs by the author unless otherwise credited.

Published by Van Nostrand Reinhold Company
A Division of Litton Educational Publishing, Inc.
450 West 33rd Street, New York, N.Y. 10001

Published simultaneously in Canada
by Van Nostrand Reinhold Ltd.

16   15   14   13   12   11   10   9   8   7   6   5   4

Contents

I. Stages of Development

A. PRESCHOOL STITCHERY

A child's first impulse to stitch may strike around 3 years old or even younger. He is likely to be able to handle a needle when he has been "scribbling" with crayons for a few weeks. The important thing for the mother or teacher is to be ready for the moment when the child wants to stitch so that an immediate start can be made and the precious impulse is not lost. The moment may well come when a child is watching someone sewing. Small children love to imitate grownups. A mother or grandmother quietly stitching creates an atmosphere of security, and security is the constant concern of childhood. "Sewing" together can be the beginning of an intensely satisfying rapport. A mother who makes time each day to listen patiently to a 4-year-old's lively chatter will create a channel of communication which will become increasingly valuable as the years roll by, especially in adolescence.

Ideally, a preschool child should begin to stitch if and when HE or SHE is ready and eager to do so. (Henceforth, for the sake of simplicity HE will be used as a generic term meaning SHE as much as HE.)

Avoid long preliminaries: the creative spirit is elusive — be ready for the moment when it strikes. The necessary material should be ready and taut, the needle threaded and anchored, ready to go. Offering choices of materials and colors should be avoided the first time. Choosing is apt to be confusing for a preschool child. Decisions take time, and delays may cause the first impulse to be lost along the way.

When the child is very young, 2¹/₂ or 3 years old, quietly and quickly solve problems beyond his grasp, otherwise he may drop everything. Then let him continue what he was doing so that the continuity is not broken. For instance, if the needle becomes unthreaded, rethread and anchor it for him until he is able to do it for himself.

As the child's understanding and manipulative skill increases, show him on a separate cloth what causes a problem. (I call this piece of cloth a "doodling cloth" because, just as some people doodle with pen and pencil, I like to doodle with a needle.) Lead him to win his own battle rather than win it for him. If he is struggling with a physical problem such as yarn tangling, give only the help needed to solve the immediate problem. Show him how to let the needle and thread dangle straight down and unwind, gently sliding the thumb and index finger down along the thread. The child must be free from the labored traditional approach which so frequently kills creativity. What is important is not the result in terms of adult esthetics, rather, it should be simply the act and the child's joy of "doing"; it should be the experience, the delight of discovery, the process of learning and growing.

A good plan is to vary the experiences by changing the materials. Children have a longer attention span when they are working with something new. Some children are fascinated by the precision of $1/8$-inch hardware cloth (see page 154), using it many times in preference to ordinary cloth. With other children, it is the other way around. Let the child play freely with needle and thread. It does not matter whether he starts with a knot on the front or the back. Let him stab the needle straight up and down; if the yarn catches around a corner or if it goes over and around the edge, as it probably will a few times, think of it as just a way of working stitches. It may become an edging. After a while the eye differentiates between center and edge and children usually decide to stab the needle on the side where the yarn came out (especially if they are having the experience of watching a mother sewing). Some children may need help in overcoming this hurdle. One teacher had a group of children chanting as they stitched, "Front to Back, Back to Front, Front to Back," and so on.

A preschool child's attention span is usually very short. Do everything you can so that there is no unnecessary interruption; if the experience lasts only five minutes, it is still valuable. The general impression should be that it is fun and something to try again. When you sense boredom, stop and start some other time. Some children can continue for as long as an hour. Richard (page 13), was in deep concentration for two hours.

"I sewing," said 2½-year-old Eleanor. Her first spontaneous stitches in blue, red, and green cotton yarn were tossed off quickly and joyfully, in a square frame. They show the inborn sense of design in young children.

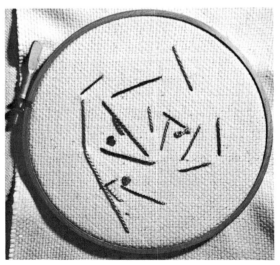

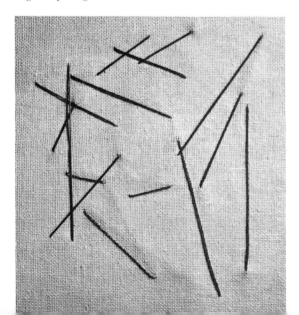

"This is a sewing," said 3-year-old Sarah. It was worked spontaneously on two-over-two monk's cloth stretched in a 6-inch hoop. She chose gold, blue, and red pearl cotton, size 3. The beginning knots are all on the front and add to the interest of the piece.

Hardware Cloth Stitching

Working with hardware cloth is fascinating for all ages (see Hardware Cloth, page 154). Some professional artists use this medium, achieving interesting designs by weaving yarns through the mesh.

Hardware cloth is a useful material for the very young child; it provides a good preliminary step to stitching on cloth. Because it is made of metal and is rigid, a needle is not necessary if the tip of the yarn has been hardened (see Needle Substitute, page 166).

A piece 6 by 9 inches with $^1/_8$-inch mesh is good for the average child and is the size he will enjoy most. If a needle is used, a tapestry needle size 17 or 18 will go through the mesh. Remember to anchor the needle (see page 18). A $^1/_4$-inch mesh is particularly suited to the very young child, $2^1/_2$ to 3 years old, and for the child with manipulative problems. A tapestry needle size 14 goes through $^1/_4$-inch mesh. Use colorful all-cotton rug yarns. For suitable yarns see page 163. Start with about a 28-inch length. Ask the child to point out where on the piece of mesh he would like to start, then tie the yarn end around a mesh for him until he can do this unaided.

All children love the security of a skill mastered. There is something soothing and comforting about the discovery of stitch progression, in and out of the mesh with colorful yarns. The learning process is simplified because the regular, firm mesh provides a definite stitching place. They may want to do the same thing many times.

Two or three pieces of hardware cloth are probably all you will need before the child is given a different material. The pieces can be used over again; children often enjoy pulling out their hardware cloth "sewing." It is just another game. Some children want more pieces; in that case vary the size to vary the experience, and provide new colors of yarn. Older children can profit and derive much enjoyment from working on large pieces. Don't forget to bind the edges (see page 154).

Quarter-inch hardware cloth stitchery by a 3-year-old girl at Junior Village, Washington, D.C. She had a wonderful time with it. For her, the "doing" was the important thing. She showed no interest in the finished piece.

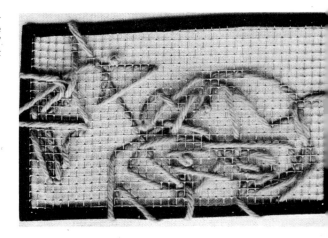

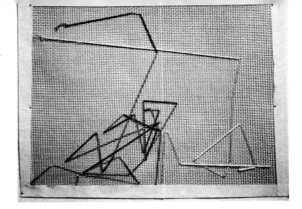

Sarah, 3 years old. Fiberglass, stitched with red, pink, and green pearl cotton. It was tossed off very quickly.

Fiberglass Screening

Another useful aid to first steps in stitching is Fiberglass screening (see page 154) because it stays reasonably taut, is light and easy to handle. Start with a piece 6 by 9 inches. Cover the edges with masking tape. As the child grows so can the size of the pieces, not only because of his ability to handle larger pieces but because he has more to express.

A yarn or string not heavier than pearl cotton size 3 or 5 can be used without a needle and go through the Fiberglass mesh if one end is treated with Elmer's glue as described on page 166. However, it is easier to work with a tapestry needle size 18 or 20, which will go through the mesh with little or no effort, depending on the thickness of the yarn used. Heavy yarns requiring real effort to pull through may discourage a child. Weights of threads such as pearl cotton in sizes 3 or 5 pull through easily with a needle. Experiment with what you have, even with twine. Remember that a slight tug for you may mean muscular tension for a child. If the child needs to make this effort as therapy, slowly increase the weight of the thread. Be sure to anchor the needle.

Canvas

Canvas is a firm open mesh material which stays stiff and prevents puckering (see page 155). It is good for young children because there is little effort need-

Left, monocanvas. Richard, 4 years old. A brown tree with green leaves on the top, and at the end of the horizontal branches. One branch thrusts out over and around the edge. A red swing attached to a branch is swinging to the left, falling down on the right!
Right, Cross Stitch canvas. An original, colorful stitchery worked with precise stitches by a 7-year-old boy from Amsterdam, in the Netherlands. It represents Peter, the little Moorish boy who is Saint Nicholas' traditional helper.

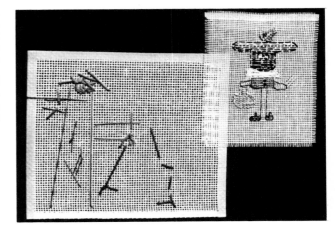

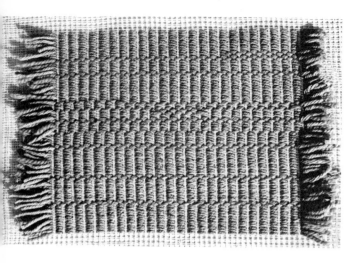

Rug canvas. A table mat by David, 6½. He used 4-ply yarn in alternating colors, turquoise blue and coral red, enjoying the relaxing precision of the canvas.

ed to push and pull the needle through. Several varieties can be used with equal success. A piece approximately 6 by 9 inches, or even smaller, would be adequate for the first attempt. Run masking tape around the back or over the edge, to prevent raveling.

The size of the canvas holes determines the size of the needle and yarn, which should go through without tugging. Four holes to the inch would require a tapestry needle size 14. Ten holes to the inch, size 18.

Stitchery on Paper and Cardboard

Let the child design his own sewing cards, even if it is only a wandering line scribbled with crayon. Let him try several drawings and choose the one he would like to stitch.

Start with pieces of rubberized and plasticized shelf paper about 6 by 9 inches. Later increase the size (see recommended paper, page 157). When the child is able to, and if the idea appeals to him, he can sometimes vary the rectangular shape by cutting shapes of his own and stitching in details. It could be a fish, a boat, a house. A further step would be to use the technique described on page 25, with crinoline over the paper. Use a chenille needle size 17, if the child can handle a sharp point, otherwise a tapestry needle. An embroidery or crewel needle size 1 makes piercing very easy. Use cotton such as pearl cotton size 3, or a light weight cotton rug yarn, or even soft twine. Instead of a starting knot, which might pull out, scotch tape the end of the thread on the back of the paper.

Children usually love to draw and stitch on paper. They can make book marks, birthday cards, get well cards, a table or tray mat. Red shelf-lining paper worked with white twine makes wonderful Christmas cards. The age at which a child can do this depends on when he gets a feel for not pulling so hard that the paper tears. Some children do not respond to the medium. If they don't, drop it and try something else.

Light cardboard is hard to pierce with a needle, but if a child has made a

10

Five-year-old Albertine, who lives in Amsterdam, worked this stitchery on light cardboard. She first made a drawing with pencil and crayons, then stitched it with yarns of many colors. It is delightfully spontaneous and free.

drawing and would like to enrich it with stitches, he can make holes with a pointed tool, or an adult can make holes every half inch or so, following the child's lines. If the holes are large enough, the thread-end, dipped in Elmer's glue and dried, can be used instead of a needle.

Other Materials

New materials are constantly becoming available. Investigate possibilities. Variations in approach are valuable towards a child's development. Sewing and weaving motions can be practised in many ways. The little plastic baskets in which fruits and vegetables are packaged can be used with colorful yarns to further develop manual dexterity. They can be made into delightful presents for the child to give.

2. STITCHING ON CLOTH

Just as his first expression with a crayon is scribbling lines, so will be a child's first expression on cloth with a needle and thread. He is truly "doodling with a needle" and unconsciously learning muscular control.

For the very young child, the cloth chosen should be easy to pierce, pleasant to handle, and plain, with no distracting designs on it (see Cloth, page 157). It should be inexpensive because the important point is to have many pieces available. Changes of material and color bring renewed interest.

An inexpensive 6-inch wooden hoop WITH A SCREW, or a small frame (see pages 161-162), will keep the material taut and make handling easy for small hands. It prevents frustrating puckering and helps the child to get a feel for tension of threads. For a 6-inch hoop, a 9-by-9 piece of material is large enough. Some children may be started with a hoop as young as 2½, others not until they are 3 or 4 years old.

Use heavy, but not too heavy, yarns; too much effort stifles spontaneity. (See Yarns and Needles, pages 163-164). Then, too, when children start stitching on cloth, they want to be "sewing" and not in a way that is too different from their mothers. The choice of thread colors should be limited at first to not more than four, preferably in the same weight; decisions delay the start. It is important at the very beginning to get quickly to the act of "doing," of stitching, with as few preliminaries as possible. It might even be wise to have only one color for the first stitchery, otherwise you will be asked for a new color every two or three stitches and spoil the flow. After the first time, choices of color and texture provide one of the most joyful experiences connected with stitcheries. In the beginning, thread and anchor the needle, knot the end. Later on the child can be taught to do this for himself. All this should take place in a peaceful, relaxed atmosphere: a good spot for a grandmother!

Two-and-a-Half and Three Years Old

The first spontaneous stitches of 2½-, 3- and even 4-year-olds are apt to be a collection of Straight Stitches, tossed off at random, mostly long, a few short, some crossing each other. They may be in any direction although vertical stitches usually dominate. As pointed out earlier, the child may start with a knot on the front instead of the back. Why not? Sometimes he will encircle the yarn around the hoop or over the edge or the material instead of going in on the side it came out. Most children do this at least once or twice, learning by experience, for instance, that the hoop is "trapped" and can't get away. They may be helped by the chant "Back to front, front to back" mentioned earlier. The size and number of stitches varies with the impulse of the mo-

When almost 3 years old, Andrew had his first experience with "trapped" hoops. He made his first stitchery, visible on the table, on a piece of 6-by-9 quarter-inch hardware cloth, going over and around the edges with unconcerned delight. For his second stitchery, he wanted cloth for "a sewing." He naturally repeated the same motions and was really amazed when he could not free the cloth from the hoops. After he had pondered for a while but before he could lose interest, it was suggested to him that he might pull out the stitches that kept the hoops trapped. So he pulled out several stitches and was triumphant when the hoops were freed. He handed over the cloth and hoops to be put together again — something too hard for a 3-year-old — and started again. For quite a while, before each stitch, he would look up and say questioningly: "THIS side?" He caught himself going around the hoops several times but shook his head: "Oh, oh, no!" In no time he had grasped the principle. It takes some children longer. The point is to help them only to figure out "why." Andrew's yarn was securely anchored, .which is why he can hold the needle, pulling, with his hand relaxed.

A

B

C

D

Watching a 4-year-old stitch gives a fascinating insight into his thinking processes, his imagination, and his ability to express himself creatively.

This was Richard's fourth stitchery but his first with hardware cloth (1/8-inch mesh). He was completely taken by the medium and sat for two uninterrupted hours in spite of many distractions around him, an unusually long attention span for a 4-year-old. He used five 28-inch lengths of light cotton rug yarn, working without a needle, the ends hardened with Elmer's glue, except for the last thread used.

He was just experimenting DOING, with nothing particular in mind when he started. His stitches formed an enclosed, more or less circular shape, with red yarn (A). Switching from red to white yarn, he worked stitches inside the shape (B). A thought came to him. He announced after a few stitches that this was the clothes dryer and that the clothes were tumbling inside (C). He used up the length of white yarn, then proceeded to fill the empty space between the white and red yarn with blue yarn, showing the good inborn design instinct of young children.

The clothes dryer completed, he stitched on neatly around the edge of the mesh with green yarn (fun of a new color) (D). Starting at the top right, he worked across the top, first with a few medium-sized stitches, then over one, under one, around three sides, until he ran out of thread, obviously enjoying the mechanics, the precision, and the security of a process mastered. Looking thoughtfully at his work, he sensed that there was a big empty space. Without a word, he searched in a box of threads, a definite objective in mind. He pulled out a skein of variegated cream to tan yarn, saying, "I need some of that." (This was threaded and anchored for him, using a tapestry needle, size 17, because the yarn end had not been treated with glue.) He did all this without any distracting adult chatter.

Starting at the bottom edge, stitching upward, he announced: "That's Mommy standing by the clothes dryer." Since he had had to search for cream yarn, he must have had "Mommy" in mind before he started this part of his work. The head finished, he went on up to the top and then straight down with the now familiar secure experience of over one, under one. Whether this was still part of Mommy, or to express the idea of standing, or just the joy of the restful process, he did not say at the time. Months later he volunteered that it was "Mommy's hair." As he reached the lower edge, he was called for dinner. Was the piece completed at that moment? We will never know (E).

E

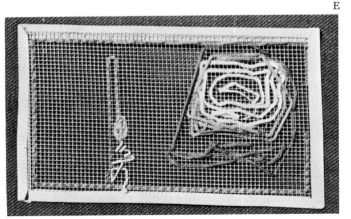

ment and the duration of the child's attention span. First stitcheries in a hoop are usually similar, whether the child is 2½, 3, or 4 years old. The shape of the hoop influences the placement of stitches.

Although the majority of children make long stitches with a few short ones, some children will from time to time make a series of small tight stitches on top of each other. The larger stitches should be encouraged with higher praise; they should not be dictated. There should be as little interference as possible. What is important is not the end product but the exhilarating experience of having created something entirely personal. "Let ME do it," "I want to do it all by self," are frequent assertions of young children. They experience pride in having produced something without help. Display the result!

Children want a new piece of cloth for a new expression just as they want a new sheet of paper for a new drawing. If possible, have a good supply of pieces of material in a variety of colors. Twelve-inch lengths in three or four different colors should provide an ample supply. In this way children can toss off as many stitcheries as they like.

At first the stitches and their direction just happen. The child is unconsciously learning to control his arms, hands, and fingers. Then comes the exciting discovery that he can consciously go up or down, left or right. He is becoming the master of his tool, which gives him pleasure and confidence.

At the first stage, between 2½ and 3½, the result represents nothing specific to him. He has no thought-out idea of what he is "sewing." The stitches are just a result of motion. It is therefore important not to ask him what it is. He is just having fun in the act of "doing." If asked, he is put on the defensive and has to invent an answer to satisfy you. It is best simply to praise his work and say how pleased you are. Abstract painters frequently express something they feel, rather than a specific pictorial image. Think of the child's stitchery as an abstraction, rather than as the representation of an object.

Four Years Old

First Visualization: Starting with a Definite Idea

At approximately the age of 4 (all ages in the book have to be approximate as children vary in their stages of development), the child's stitchery is telling a story to HIM or to HER, probably not to you. When it is completed, he occasionally announces on his own what it is about and perhaps tells a story of pure fantasy about it. He may "recognize" something in the haphazard lines, especially if he senses a "What is it?" attitude in the adult. As he stitches, he may explain what he is doing and change the description completely as he progresses. Soon, however, he has the joy of discovering that stitches can express something felt and willed by him. He is learning to control his tool and to stitch shapes that express an idea. He states before starting what he intends to picture. The result may not be recognizable to you, although it may well be a true expression of what he had in mind. He will frequently give you the key by spontaneously naming what he has done.

This is followed by a stage when you will be able to see what the child is able to depict because it will be closer to reality, a joyful step for the adults. Some children reach this stage soon after they are 3 or 4 years old, others not until 5. After 5, children usually have the pleasure of knowing they can express what they feel and see and can communicate their ideas to others.

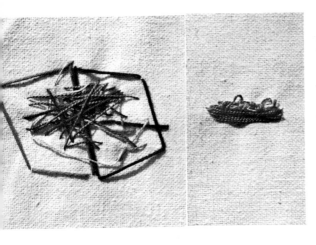

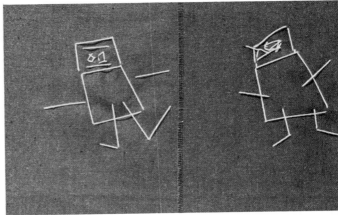

Benjamin and Alexander are 4¹/₂-year-old fraternal twins. The subject of this first set of stitcheries made in 6-inch hoops was not announced ahead of time. When the boys were through, each "recognized" something in the haphazard lines. Benjamin, left, made up a long story: "It's boats all tied up together because a man fell off the black boat." Alexander, right, said: "It's a ferry freighter."

Another day, the boys built a snowman outside the dining-room window. When it was dark and they had to come inside, they decided to make a snowman stitchery. They chose a dark blue homespun fabric and white cotton yarn.

Eleanor, age 4¹/₂, using a hoop, started with a definite idea: "It's a garden with flowers inside and a fence around it."

Five Years Old

Five-year-olds are usually eager to learn. If they have not previously had the opportunity to "sew," this is a good time to start because 5-year-olds enjoy activities centered around the home and their mother. It is a good age to develop the mother and child relationship by "sewing" together. Successful students usually come from homes where parents have shared their children's activities. Anything that will bring about a happy attitude in the child, a warm rapport with parents and teachers, a good reaction to creative manual expression is to be encouraged. Many personality traits in children evolve during the first 5 years of life.

Five-year-olds want to know how to do things and because of this are apt to want to copy. They may not be imaginative. The emphasis should be on spontaneous work, on the excitement of a new skill, on the act of "doing." Share the fun with them. It is particularly important at this stage to resist the temptation of starting out by teaching specific stitches, of showing how, because the child may well ask to be shown how. Don't do for him what he should be doing for himself. Only show how if there is no other way and do it on a separate piece of cloth. As much as possible, let the experience be the thrill of discovery, of what he can do on his own as needs arise. It should be fun with no attempt at perfection.

Five is a good time to provide a suitable choice of color and texture. The rate of progress depends a great deal on the number of stitcheries worked by the child. Each one is a step forward and improvement comes fast. If you always have cut pieces of materials, yarns, and needles in a box, ready to use when the desire strikes, you will get better results, especially if you are working on your own stitchery and obviously enjoying it. Encourage the child to talk about what he has done; not "What is it?" but "Tell me about it." As he experiences the medium, you have the opportunity to enlarge his vocabulary, his sense of feel with texture such as smooth and rough, his sense of color — not only naming colors, but, as he grows in understanding, comparisons such as dark, medium, and light, warm and cool.

3. STIMULATING THE IMAGINATION OF THE PRESCHOOL CHILD

Most children have wonderful imaginations but some may need help to find ways of expressing themselves with needle and thread, instead of crayons.

Inspiration for a 5-year-old could come from "taking a walk with stitches." It is fun to think of stitches walking quietly, then suddenly running, going along a straight road, then a curving road, turning at the end of the road, perhaps skipping up and down, taking long steps, little steps. This type of stitching does not require much concentration. The child could be sitting up in bed, or sitting in a corner of the kitchen chatting away about all the things he might see during his imaginary walk. You can have two people going on the walk, using a second color for the second person. One could be walking along straight lines (mother) while the other skipped along; or it could be a child and his dog, with little stitches to show the dog running off, and coming back. A child could express the rhythm of a song — long and short notes in long and short stitches. This can turn into a guessing game — what song is this? Another idea might be to think of water running and splashing, of a bird flying, railroad tracks. This type of exercise stimulates a child's imagination, helps him to develop the faculty of giving concrete form to feeling and thought.

Ideas could spring from the reading of a short story such as Jack and Jill. Japanese haiku poems appeal to children; they suggest rather than describe, leaving much to the imagination. Sometimes a word will start a train of thought: a dragon fly, a caterpillar, a sunflower, stick people, make-believe animals.

Taking a walk with stitches.

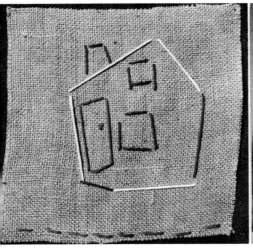 

Five-year-old John was given a piece of gold bur-lap stiffened with tissue pasted on the back with light rubber latex. He threaded his own size **14** needle after the soap treatment (see below), an-chored it, and in a few minutes joyfully tossed off his first stitchery. He announced ahead of time that he was going to make a picture of his house. There was no talk about stitches or what to do — he just went ahead on his own. There was one point he stressed, the last stitch, his punch line, so to speak: the knob on the door. John wanted reassurance that everyone would notice it.

Right:
Tea cozy. A Christmas present. The tree by Elea-nor, age 5. The other side by Richard, age 3, is decorated with a series of random stitches.

Children love the opportunity to make rather than buy gifts; they will love to add stitches on the pocket of an apron for mother or grandmother, or on a pocket for the child's own dress, a table mat for father's breakfast. A little 4-year-old girl made a table mat for her father with three fuzzy worms in the center; she said, "It will be such fun for Daddy to squish them under his plate every morning."

4. THREADING AND ANCHORING THE NEEDLE, KNOTTING THE END

Threading the Needle

Easy threading of the needle makes a great difference in the attitude of chil-dren towards stitchery. A small bar of dry soap cut in two will pay untold dividends.

Using a 28- to 30-inch length of yarn, cut one end straight across and moisten it between your lips. Place one half of the soap on a table and on it lay an inch or so (not too much) of the moistened end of the yarn. Place the second piece of soap on top, pressing very firmly with your right hand. The thread is sandwiched between the two pieces of soap. With your left hand, hold the yarn up and draw out. Repeat two or three times. The soap leaves a coating on the thread that stiffens it and makes it slide easily through the eye of the needle. For wool and heavy cotton yarns, the process should be re-

A

B

John, age 5, drawing out the cotton rug yarn between two pieces of soap.

Guiding the stiffened and flattened yarn through
the eye of the needle.

peated several times. If you have only one small piece of soap, place the
thread on a hard surface, lay the soap on top and repeat the above process
on both sides of the thread. Make sure that the eye of the needle is large
enough to accommodate the thread and that the eye is as long as in tapestry
needles (see Needles, page 164).

To thread the needle, hold the soap-treated end of the thread between the
CUSHIONS of the left-hand thumb and index finger, not the nails. The
thread should barely show between the cushions of the fingers. Practice
pressing the finger tips together and then relaxing them, so that the thread
alternately shows or does not show between the cushions of the fingers.
With the thread in the left hand barely showing, hold the needle in the right
hand close to the eye of the needle. Place the eye over the thread, easing and
guiding the thread right through the eye. As the thread emerges from the eye,
grasp the needle in the left hand and pull completely through with the right
thumb and index finger. The stiffened and flattened thread will slide through
easily.

If soap is not available, moisten the end of the yarn and flatten it between
your fingers.

Another method for threading wool yarn which has not been given the
soap treatment is to hold the needle in your right hand, the yarn in your
left hand. Fold about an inch of the end of the yarn down over the eye of
the needle, holding it tightly between the cushions of the thumb and index
finger. Slide the needle out. Press the eye down over the folded edge of yarn.
The yarn should be peeking through. Then hold the needle in the left hand.
Pull the yarn through the eye with the right hand.

Left-handed children should reverse the whole process, starting with the
yarn in the right hand, the needle in the left.

With little practice small children triumphantly thread needles, a wonderful exercise in concentration and coordination. Give them two pieces of soap
in a plastic bag to keep with their stitchery supplies.

Anchoring the Needle

Too frequently, when a child is concentrating on stitching, the needle pulls
off the thread. This is not only frustrating, it also slows down the initial impulse. Hanging on to the yarn and needle too tightly, so that the yarn will not

C

D

Splitting the yarn in two with the point of the needle.

The needle is anchored and it won't come off. It's magic! (Photographs A, B, C, D by Don Normark.)

slip off, often cramps small fingers, which is not desirable. The hand should be relaxed.

The anchoring process gives children who master it a great sense of accomplishment. It is an invaluable aid to mothers, and to many a willing teacher who had to forego the fruitful classroom experience of stitchery because she couldn't keep up with 30 needles constantly unthreaded. It is invaluable with the handicapped of all ages.

Children learn the process easily. They love doing it. There is magic in it! It can be used with yarns that have some twist to them such as cotton rug yarns, pearl cottons, wools. It should not be attempted with fine sewing threads, which cannot be easily split, or with stranded yarns, cotton or wool, which do not have a real twist.

First thread the needle (see Threading the Needle, soap treatment, page 17), drawing out a tail about 4 inches long for average needles, 5 or 6 inches for long needles such as size 14. Holding the middle of the needle in the right hand, the long end of the thread in the left, split the yarn in TWO with the point of the needle, at a place just about the length of the needle. Be careful that the yarn is split exactly in two. For instance, if you are working with four-ply rug yarn, the needle should split the yarn so that two threads are on each side. Even tension is the magic that does it. With your right hand, gently push the needle almost through. Then pick it up by the point and pull it completely through the split yarn. Hold on to the short end of the thread to be sure it is not also pulled through the split yarn. You will find that the needle is firmly anchored. (See page 151: how anchoring the needle was discovered.)

Knotting the End

Children can be taught to knot the end of the yarn by wrapping it three times around the index finger of the right hand, twisting it between the finger and the thumb, pulling it off, then sliding it between thumb and index finger to the end. Another way is to make a circle with the yarn around the index finger of your left hand, slip it off and wrap the short end over and under two or three times, then pull into a knot.

For a time, a mother or teacher may have to secure the end of the yarn just used while the child threads, anchors, and knots the next length.

B. SCHOOL AGE STITCHERY

Stitchery in a class is a challenge to the inventive teacher. How different the approach is today from the strictly supervised exact stitches of past generations with the deadening effects of enforced conformity. Today's children learn through discovery. The stress is not on technique but on motivating and stimulating each child to explore so that he will grow to his full potential as an individual. Technical competence comes amazingly quickly when a child is inspired. If he has a need — such as how to express a certain texture with stitches — he often creates what he needs with little if any help, and this is good. I constantly come across "new" stitches "invented" by children. Give each child a doodling cloth on which he can doodle with a needle, experiment and learn. It will help him to develop freedom with stitches. Look up page 157 for suitable cloths.

Mothers or teachers who have not stitched before will find that a good way for them to start is to learn and practice a few basic stitches on a doodling cloth of their own. The stitches that are starred in the Index would provide a good beginning.

School-age stitcheries should be directed towards individual spontaneous creative expression; children love it and have a fresh naïve approach that is most appealing. Large classes can be divided into small groups with the teacher working with one group at a time. In a group, the children will influence each other. They learn from one another. The child who has stitched at home is apt to be a helpful leader who will inspire others. Those who lack confidence and tend to imitate the others are the ones who need most to have their creativity developed. They may need to be asked simple questions to bring the original idea back into focus. One possible way to cope with the problem of children imitating each other's work is to suggest that each one start with a secret idea, possibly whispered to the teacher, to surprise the class. It will help if they sit silently, their eyes closed, "thinking" their very own picture, different from anyone else's, making it come from deep inside, a personal experience. The size of their piece should be such that they can easily complete it. The first creative impulse should be directed to the main part of the work. Much initial enthusiasm is lost if a child is expected to hem or bind the edges. After they have made a start, encourage them to fill the space; also to look upon their stitchery as something they can pick up during free intervals, working a few stitches each time.

Children should not be stifled with demands for perfection of stitches. Let them find their own way. When they need help, be there as a consultant, as a source of information. Encourage relaxed stitches. If a stitch looks tight, sliding the needle under it and easing it up slightly helps to loosen it. If the need for the mechanics of a stitch arises, a piece of thin white cardboard with large stitches worked by the teacher in colorful cotton rug yarns can be shown to a whole class and passed around from hand to hand. Leave the last stitch loose, unfinished, to give a better idea of how the stitch was made. A piece of heavily starched burlap could be used in the same manner. Many teachers in later grades make up large samplers of a few basic stitches and pin them up, to be consulted. When a basic stitch is mastered and the children show interest in it, a successful approach is to encourage them to find as many variations of that stitch as they can and share their findings with

Stitchery

Running
Whipped Running
Back Stitch
Couching
Satin
Blanket
Buttonhole

Feather
Cross
Sheaf or Bundle
Star
Chain
Square Chain

Detached Chain
French Knot

A chart of basic stitches for third grade students, by Gladys Finley.

the others. After this the teacher may want to show one or two additional examples.

As soon as children are old enough, let them follow the diagram of a needed stitch in this book, much as they learn to look up words in the dictionary; let it be a process of discovery. When an individual child has a problem with a stitch, show him on a SEPARATE doodling cloth, not on his own piece. If you work on his piece, he will be quick to compare and see the disparity between his proficiency and yours. This is discouraging. He is also apt to be like a mother bird whose fledgeling has been handled by human hands: she loses interest in him. A good practice is to show on your own cloth that there may be several ways of expression. Suggest that the child might find a way of his own — and so frequently he does! If something strikes you as a problem, let the child try to take care of it, as much as possible, remembering that at that stage the result does not really matter as long as he is satisfied with it. It is the "doing" that counts. Improvement comes with practice.

Until the 6- or 7-year-old child reaches sufficient muscular control and understanding to pull the yarn without puckering the cloth, it is well to stiffen limp material such as burlap. Even adults find this helpful. (See page 160.) Most children do their best work with the material stretched on a simple frame the size of the stitchery they planned (see page 162); it makes the stitching easier and, because it is mounted and has a professional look, they respond and stretch their ability to the utmost.

Besides yarns provided by the schools, each child can bring left-over yarns from home, especially from the third grade on. One short length of thread might be exactly what one child needs for a special effect. This will open their eyes to varieties in textures and colors with ideas springing from the materials at hand. Their stitcheries and treasures, with spare needles and scissors, can be kept in individual shoe boxes. Being uniform in size, these boxes, marked with each child's name, can be stacked neatly on a shelf.

Encourage children to work spontaneously on cloth. Many of them will feel the need of a preliminary sketch on a piece of paper; it gives them confidence in planning the filling of space. They can then repeat the outline on the material with chalk, crayon, or a nylon-tip pen, using a minimum of lines. It is good for children to learn that a picture THEY have drawn can be expressed over again on cloth with needle and thread, although it need not be exactly the same. Let them repeat their own drawing free hand. Anything can be expressed in stitches. If they feel the need of transferring, there is a way described on page 163. Reproduce the drawing for the child only if he is really not able to or if he is anxious that you should. (Read about Kim below.)

It is important to remember that it is best to work directly on the cloth. This is what the Peruvian children of Chijnaya did when they started out to stitch scenes from their village at the suggestion of Peace Corps volunteers. They had no paper on which to draw, so they thought about what they wanted to stitch, carried a general picture in their minds, and went ahead on the cloth, inventing details as they went along. It is also what the Egyptian children of Harrania did: as they wove on their looms, they let the yarns speak. Free expression by the children is the keynote of Professor Wassef's experiment. The more steps there are between the original feeling and the expression, the more chance there is that the spark will be lost.

In the classroom, teachers have many opportunities to create an atmosphere that will stimulate their pupils and lead to original self expression. The quality and the intensity of the stimulation will determine the quality of

The five-legged deer by a tree was drawn with color crayon by Eleanor at age 6. The drawing and colors used were so delightful that I could not resist embroidering it myself for a cushion, reproducing as faithfully as possible the texture of the crayon strokes. Let children design for you — but not the reverse! This is a good exercise for an adult, to develop a sensitivity to the use of stitches.

Ten-year-old Kim is Korean born. She came to the United States when she was four. Her adoptive mother writes: "The carry-over of Kim's oriental heritage in her art work has been interesting." It is indeed fascinating to see how Korean the piece is — the design, the colors, the whole feeling — especially the figure to the left in national dress.

Kim tossed off the drawing on an old cut-up manila folder, with no thought of stitchery. At that time there was a general enthusiasm for stitchery running through the household of five girls. Kim's aunt, admiring the spontaneous drawing, suggested to her that she transfer it to cloth for a stitchery. Kim liked the idea and was eager to express her drawing with stitches but she could not be interested in the actual process of transferring to cloth. If urged too much, she would have lost interest, as she is easily discouraged. Her drawing was reproduced by her aunt with remarkable integrity. Kim took it from there, working effortlessly on her own, choosing her own colors and making up stitches as she went along. It is a delightful, very Korean piece.

A boy in Chijnaya, Peru, working on his stitchery. The cloth is local homespun wool woven by the women of the village. The children use bright-colored yarns and so far have used Chain Stitch almost entirely to outline and fill the shapes. The sale of the stitcheries through the Andean Foundation makes it possible for the children to buy shoes and school supplies. (Courtesy of the Andean Foundation, Clifton, Virginia.)

On the banks of Lake Titicaca. The Chijnaya embroideries show the remarkable instinctive sense of design and color used by the boys and girls, whose ages range from 6 to 16. I find their work irresistible. (From the author's collection.)

Eight-year-old Julie is a very talented little girl who sketches with needle and yarn as freely as with pencil or paint brush. How we wish we could do as well in any medium! Her spontaneous little dogs are so alive they literally jump out of the picture.

the result. A teacher who is personally involved in stitchery is apt to carry his or her enthusiasm into the classroom. If the teacher is on fire, the class will really light up.

Ideas for stitcheries at school might arise from studies of such subjects as animals, plants, the seashore, rockets and space craft, social studies, a period in history, a study of another country, special occasions such as Columbus Day, the Fourth of July, a visit to the zoo, to a farm. Nature is an endless source of inspiration: flowers, leaves, grasses, seed pods, mosses, mushrooms, shells; or, failing the real thing, good reproductions. (A magnifying glass is very useful to focus on the beauty of a detail.) Let these things, coming from a personal experience and familiarity with the subject, suggest designs and textures, not by copying nature but by expressing a response to what has been observed, interpreting with yarns and fabric as spontaneously as possible, with emphasis on individuality. As Charles Gaitskell said so well in *Children and Their Art:* "Artistic expression worthy of the name reflects the thoughts and feelings of its author ... it never emerges from a void." There is something fresh, direct, and free, an intuitive quality in children which shows through in their stitcheries. It should be allowed to grow and blossom.

How do you stimulate a child at home so that he will want to stitch? Example is the best way. Your chances of success are much greater if you yourself are stitching. As you work on your doodling cloth, children will be attracted and look at what seems obviously enjoyable; they will become interested in stitches. Suggest that they explore and experiment on a doodling cloth of their own. Create an enthusiastic climate, give them confidence in expressing themselves. Working with a small group is a great help.

As students become older and more experienced, they are better able to appreciate textiles and draw inspiration from decorated fabrics of the past. They should be shown reproductions of creative stitcheries. Textile collections in museums and illustrations in museum publications are an endless source of design material; school children benefit greatly from visiting museums and from viewing slides of textiles and other works of art which illustrate good design. Those who have learned to create with stitches may develop into stitchery artists and in turn make a contribution to the "Threads of History."

SIX YEARS OLD

A 6-year-old's stitchery is apt to be direct and spontaneously realistic. He likes to stitch animals, a house with a tree besides it, a sun in the sky. He can be taught to thread and anchor the needle. If he has trouble, in spite of the

Robert, age 6, worked this landscape with neat stitches, using a 6-inch hoop. It is typical of that age, well balanced, with sun and sky.

soap treatment described on page 17, give him a larger needle; size 14 should handle almost any yarn. He understands quickly that the threads usually start and end on the back of the cloth.

The 6-year-old finds decisions difficult. If you give him a wide choice of weights of yarn, such as thick and thin, hoping he will choose the thick yarn, which will give a fuller effect, he is very apt to make the wrong choice and consequently be disappointed with the results. Let choices be among equally suitable materials, such as a good weight of thread for the material at hand. When he is older and has more manipulative experience, at approximately 8 years old, he will also have more understanding; a choice can be reasonably discussed with him so that he can learn to make his own decisions successfully.

In the first grade he likes to work at his project while others around him are doing the same thing. At home he will enjoy stitching with his mother, if she too is stitching. His attention span is short, partly because he tires easily. Don't force him or let him reach saturation point; a few stitches a day may be all he can do.

First Grade Stitchery (Eastgate School, Bellevue, Washington.)
(See Color page 27, C-2, 3, 4, 5, 6.)

Nina Barkauskas was eager to give to her first grade class of 30 children the experience of drawing and painting with needle and thread. The children were encouraged to draw on paper, bold clear drawings with definite lines, using color crayons or paints. Each child drew whatever he wanted on paper sizes varying roughly from 8 by 9 inches to 9 by 12 inches. Cotton crinoline was placed over the drawings and stapled around the edges. (An improvement would be nylon crinoline. See page 157.) If there is no stapler, use masking tape or anything that will hold paper and crinoline together. Some children chose colored nylon net instead of crinoline, but the latter proved more satisfactory. It was transparent, so the drawing showed through, and firm enough to keep the paper taut, yet it was pliable. The children chose their own yarns to outline and accent the drawings. Some used white twine, coloring it later with crayons. They were given large needles, No. 14, with a sharp point, sometimes referred to as chenille or couching needles. An embroidery or crewel needle No. 1 would pierce the crinoline and paper more easily. Most of them could thread the needles, a few had to be helped. The first time, the teacher threaded several needles before class to avoid delays. The children were shown how to anchor the thread so that it would not pull out, and how to knot the end.

Stitching through paper and crinoline, the children first used Running Stitches to outline the shapes. For some it was easy. Others had a short attention span or coordination difficulties and worked only a few stitches each day. As the need arose, the teacher demonstrated to small groups on a separate piece of cloth how each stitch was worked, helping children individually when they had difficulty with a stitch. Some children helped each other. They learned to work Running Stitches in zigzag, also to Whip and Lace them effectively. They discovered Straight Stitches. Straight Stitches close together became Satin Stitches. They learned the Back Stitch and the Blanket Stitch. Improvement came quickly. Several children used Blanket Stitches for the ground, around flowers and edges. A few of them, not all, were able to make Chain Stitches and French Knots.

Color Illustrations

C-1. Andrew, age 3, tossed off his fourth stitchery in ten minutes, choosing for it red burlap on a 9-by 12-inch frame. The needle was threaded and anchored, the ends knotted for him. Apart from this no help was given or requested, no suggestions made. Young children frequently have an in-born sense of balance and design. (See "Designing with Stitches," page 131.)

C-2. Kirstene's sun and flowers were first drawn and colored on paper. She chose green nylon net to be stapled over the paper. Kirstene had difficulty in coordinating. This was a very useful exercise for her and meant a real effort. (See First Grade, page 25.)

C-3. Mary's delightful giraffe was first drawn and colored on paper over which crinoline was stapled. She "invented" Satin Stitches for the spots, using white twine which she colored orange with crayon to make the spots brighter. Around the sun she tried what she thought were Blanket Stitches, not too successfully, but she mastered the process for the ground. Her butterfly was worked with Buttonhole Stitches — she was learning to work the Blanket Stitch close together. She and several of the children in the class learned to make French Knots in groups for flowers. (See First Grade, page 25.)

C-4. Lisa's flying bird has real personality. It is just coming in for a landing. She has learned how to express spontaneous feeling. The drawing on paper was covered with dark blue nylon net. Most of the bird is heavily covered with Chain Stitches. (See First Grade, page 25.)

C-5. Jay chose pink nylon net to staple over his giraffe drawing. He outlined it with orange Running Stitches which were Whipped and Threaded with deep pink wool. The piece was framed with an over-the-edge stitch in orange 6-stranded cotton, a difficult type of thread which he managed unusually well. The last touch was to tie a free white wool tail on the back. (See First Grade, page 25.)

C-6. Janice's lion is delightfully spontaneous. It was first drawn on paper with color crayons. Over this a piece of crinoline was stapled. When her stitching was completed, she reinforced the colors by painting on the crinoline. The whole thing was done quickly, in two or three periods. Most of the children in the class took four or five periods. (See First Grade, page 25.)

C-1. Andrew, age 3.

C-2. Kirstene, age 6.

C-3. Mary, age 6.

C-4. Lisa, age 6.

C-5. Jay, age 6.

C-6. Janice, age 6.

Owen, with his dog on a leash, shows unusual observation for a 6-year-old. The dog is pulling the boy — something Owen has really experienced. After the crinoline was stapled on his drawing, Owen outlined it with Running Stitches with white twine doubled. He filled in his dog with brown wool Satin Stitches and colored the rest with crayon on the crinoline.

When the stitching was completed, a few children felt that the colors of their drawings did not show through enough so they colored the cotton crinoline.

Some of those who had used nylon net found that their paper had torn off in parts. The net did not hold the paper as taut as the crinoline. (The damaged part of the paper was cut off, the net and remaining drawing stapled to a different background, providing an interesting variation.) The tearing of the paper is what led me to experiment with suitable papers, and I found that although any good, strong paper will do, the rubberized, plasticized shelf paper I describe on page 157 is best.

A further step might be to incorporate beads to enhance an effect, or even small macaroni pieces, which can be colored. Pieces of fabric can be appliquéd, dried weeds couched on. Suggest materials the child can collect and use — with moderation! Stimulate his imagination, guiding him along to find his own way of expressing himself.

SEVEN YEARS OLD

Stitcheries of 7-year-old children are usually quite different from the 6-year-old's. Seven is a satisfying age for stitchery. The children quickly discover what can be done with needle and thread, taking technique in their stride. They are fascinated by the mechanics of the craft, can be absorbed for long periods, and like to finish what they have started. If they have had no previous experience, let them feel their way on a small doodling cloth. Let them find out for themselves how to start and how not to pull too much. If they need to "know how" about a stitch, their doodling cloth is a good place to try to discover how to express what they want. Doodling cloths often turn into an interesting sampler, reverting to the original meaning of the word: a record of stitches learned. If they need help, show them on your own doodling cloth, in groups of three or four, or let them look at the diagram in the book. The habit of looking up how a stitch is made can be started at this age.

Encouraging free expression continues to be paramount. They are still happily spontaneous with no self-consciousness about their work. Like the 6-year-olds, they can illustrate just about anything they want. An intuitive sense of design, a good use of space, balance and color distribution make many 7-year-old's stitcheries a delight. Years ago, 7 was an age when little girls were expected to sit for hours, working tediously on adult imposed designs. Today, stitcheries not only develop manual dexterity and coordination, they also help children to grow in artistic consciousness, encouraging tangible expression of a feeling, of an idea.

The average 7-year-old can learn to work relaxed stitches so that the stiffened material will not pucker. It is a good age to start the use of light-weight frames which can be made at home. (See Frames, page 162.) A frame is conducive to a well-designed piece because the picture can be thought of as a whole; children can see that their stitchery will be ready to hang as soon as they are through. From time to time, hold the pieces up against the wall so that the effect of their work can be seen as a whole.

Encourage them to work their stitches well enough so that the final effect will not be spoiled; they usually like to make stitches that look good to them! Seven-year-olds who have had previous experience with needle and thread become conscious of what stitches can do, how textures can be achieved. They are growing in sensitivity and awareness. The more they have learned to express their feelings from within in drawing and painting, the easier it becomes for them to do the same thing with needle and thread, working directly on the cloth, filling the space with beautiful lines and shapes as they go along, responding unconsciously to the demands of the materials at hand.

Seven-year-old Susan learned the mechanics of stitches on a separate piece of gold burlap which became her first sampler.

The freedom Susan acquired on her sampler enabled her to work her landscape directly on the cloth, drawing with the needle. The flowers are particularly free and charming, in variegated blue, yellow, and pink. The butterfly is recognizable by its two black antennae. The mountains are outlined in purple with white freehand Cross Stitch for snow.

29

C-7. Kathy, age 8.

C-8. Eleanor, age 7½.

C-9. Minor, age 8.

C-10. Steve, age 8.

C-11. Elaine, age 7.

C-12. Theresa M., age 7.

Color Illustrations

C-7. This was Kathy's first stitchery. She just wanted to make a pretty picture as a present to a very dear friend. It is an imaginary house which she first drew on paper, then redrew freehand on the burlap stretched on a frame. It was her own choice of colors, yarns, and stitches: the work of a happy, carefree child. Kathy had a wonderful time doing it. (Courtesy of Mrs. Joan Toggitt.)

C-8. My "Magination" garden by Eleanor, was worked unaided in three periods on three consecutive days. It was entirely spontaneous, worked freehand with nothing predrawn. The fact that the burlap was stretched on a permanent light frame, 12-by-10 inches, that the picture was already framed, so to speak, was of great psychological value, and a strong incentive to finish the piece.

She began with three long green stitches to express the ground, undoubtedly deduced that they were too long because, in her own words, "I figured out how to stake them down." ("I figured out" is a wonderful step in the learning process.) She then started on the flowers, completing each one before working on the next one.

Eleanor asked how she could make "a neat knot." A French Knot (see page 114) was demonstrated to her on a doodling cloth. The process delighted her. With a great sense of accomplishment she proceeded to teach French Knots to anyone willing to learn. If she had been taught unrelated French Knots, just to learn how to make them, the child would probably not have concentrated, and the learning process would have been slow. But she had a specific need, really concentrated to fill that need, learning quickly and well.

C-9. Minor said he just went ahead, drawing an imaginary bee right on the burlap with a crayon without a preliminary sketch — probably why the bee is so delightfully spontaneous. (See Third Grade, page 33.)

C-10. "This is a feeler bug, some kind of a bug I thought up." Steve drew directly on the burlap and first outlined the bug in Double Running Stitch. He filled the shape with Satin Stitches. He added clouds at the end because "something was sort of needed there." (Instinctive balance.) (See Third Grade, page 33.)

C-11. Elaine's landscape shows mastery of the medium, an unusually precise and orderly effect for a second grader. It is an excellent example of Pattern Darning, picking up one thread of the burlap so as to form a design. For the flowers and the butterfly, pink variegated yarn was used, which gives pleasing variation — a sophisticated effect in its simplicity. (See Second Grade, page 32.)

C-12. Theresa M. drew with a needle just the way a child draws with crayon at age 7. The whole scene is alive and happy. It shows a good sense of balance and space. The little girl is well placed in relation to her environment. She is on her way, holding a bag. The hair is particularly free. (See Second Grade, page 32.)

Second Grade Stitchery (Hillaire School, Bellevue, Washington.)
(See Color Page 30, C-11, 12.)

The children in Suzanne Perkins' second grade class of 34 children talked about what they would like to stitch. With crayons, each made a sketch on paper to find out how to fill the space provided by 10-inch square pieces of burlap in a choice of colors. Most of them redrew their pictures freehand on the burlap. A few worked directly on the cloth without any outline. The stitches, which developed as they were needed, were: Straight Stitches, Running Stitches, Zigzag Running, Back Stitch, Satin, Chain, Detached Chain, Feather, Cross Stitch, Couching, and French Knots. Several of the children used variegated yarns which added interest to their pieces.

Sheri's butterfly on black burlap was worked freehand with Couched heavy rug yarn. She shows how a 7-year-old can be in control of her medium.

Dean's owl on a branch was worked freehand on black burlap. The outline, head and wings, are worked in Chain Stitch in white wool with a thin silky thread. This gives a slight shimmer which is well suited to the subject. The body is filled with Zigzag Darning Stitch in three soft shades of yellow, blue, and orange alternately. It shows a great deal of care and feeling — a most appealing piece.

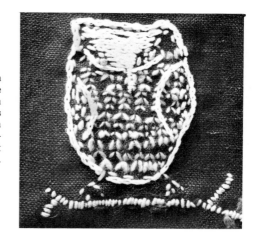

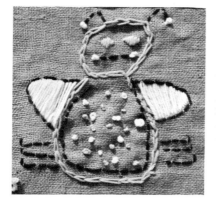

Jennifer's bug has personality. The shape was drawn directly on orange burlap with the legs going down. However, as she stitched the child must have felt that she was running out of space, so she balanced her picture by working legs freehand on the sides. I wonder if running out of space at the top is what bent the antennae!

Eight-year-olds want their stitchery to be done quickly, tossed off in one or two sittings. That very speed often gives their work good spontaneous motion. They are apt to introduce humour in their stitcheries and to stitch funny animals and bugs! They are not too concerned with finishing if they are not in the mood. They are more likely to stitch at school, when all the others in their class are stitching too, than at home. Encourage them to work directly on the material, if possible without any or with very little preliminary drawing, using quick and easy stitches, keeping alert and responsive to what is taking place under their fingers. Let the material and yarns speak to them and suggest forms of decoration. Encourage their collecting urge; they can look for yarns, strings, little scraps of material which they can use in their stitchery. This will lead them to experiment with threads of different colors, textures, and weights, laying them beside the stitches they have just worked, eliminating those that are not pleasing, finding out which colors go well together. They will discover that couching is the best way to utilize very heavy yarns like roving. They can investigate the various ways this can be achieved and experience spontaneous designing, breaking up space with lines, filling spaces with stitches to create textures.

In class, studies of other countries and other times provides ready motivation for stitchery projects. These same studies lead to maps which usually fascinate 8-year-olds. They might be interested in a stitchery map of the neighborhood. In order to develop the creative processes, it is important to use a positive approach with the 8-year-olds and to show real interest in their work. They are becoming increasingly aware of not being able to draw realistically. It is a crucial time for creativity, a time when the spontaneity of childhood may go into decline.

Since children at this age like to work in a group, at home a group project, such as provided by the Scouts, Camp Fire, Sunday School, or a neighborhood group of children, is more likely to succeed than a child working alone. Children at this age still need encouragement and praise, especially from their mothers.

Third Grade Stitchery (Three Points School, Bellevue, Washington)
(See Color Page 30, C-9, 10.)

In Gladys Finley and Carolyn Martin's third grade classes, interest in stitchery came from a need. The class was studying the history of American pioneers crossing the country in covered wagons. The children built a model covered wagon complete with pioneers and oxen, and spontaneously proceeded to decorate the hood with Running Stitches. In dressing the dolls, they felt that the dresses, too, needed to be decorated. This led to a lively discussion of stitches and how they could be used to make the clothes more authentic and interesting. They became intrigued with the whole subject of stitches and asked if they couldn't learn some. Mrs. Finley had in an indirect way created a need and was ready to fill it. She made up a chart of stitches (see page 21) and each child tried to see how many he could master. For this they each had a practice piece of burlap.

Learning stitches was no problem; the children were very eager. After a few sessions, they thought it would be a new experience to make an original stitchery. They were left completely free as to subject and use of stitches. It

David explained that this was a bug and "they make the best kind of stitchery." He didn't draw anything on either paper or burlap: "I just did it out of my head. If I drew it on the cloth and wanted to change, the lines would still be there. I first did the head, then the body and the feelers. I put stitches inside so it would look like a bug with spots. It was neat." (Meaning he loved doing it.)

The boy had had difficulty with coordination, with reading and writing. Stitchery was a joyful, easy experience for him. He was first in the class to master the stitches. His teacher related that it was through this stitchery that she felt she was reaching the child. From that time on, through this experience and the vocabulary involved, there was a marked improvement in the child's coordination, his reading and writing. Stitchery proved to be a tool towards expression and growth.

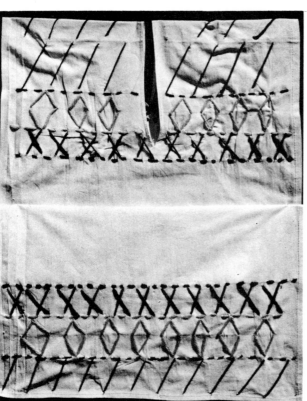

The class was studying Mexico. The children thought they would enjoy making ponchos. Ann drew lines and designs on cloth 15 inches wide and 26 inches long. She stitched over the lines and proudly wore her poncho at a school Mexican lunch. The material used was sheeting, which should be avoided because it puckers easily and has no texture.

could be anything they liked, imaginary or real. The girls tended to be realistic, several choosing flowers; the boys favored insects or imaginary bugs; a few made landscapes. Some of the children first drew their ideas on a piece of paper, with color crayons, then redrew them freehand on burlap pieces about 12 by 13 inches. Some drew directly on the burlap; a few worked

Kenny worked his stitchery completely freehand without any drawing on paper or burlap. He said he had it all pictured in his mind. He first stitched the corn, then the farmer with his hoe. After this came the background hills and the sunset.

without any crayon lines at all, holding the picture in their minds. This is good — 8-year-olds like to get going in a hurry.

Carolyn Martin is another third grade teacher in the same school. She learned stitches from Gladys Finley in the room next to hers. The contagion spread to her pupils who pleaded that they too wanted to make stitchery pictures.

NINE YEARS OLD

Nine-year-olds are realists, self-motivated individualists. They are less spontaneous than the 8-year-olds, more factual, less imaginative, and quite critical

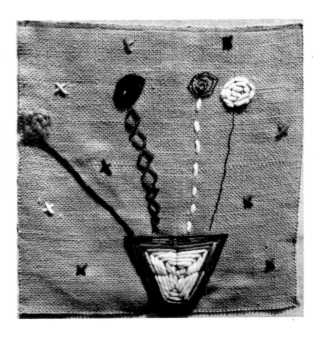

Kimberly started with the flowers. She used a different stitch for each stem "to show Mom what stitches we were learning. I'd like to know more. My aunt does some but she buys it already drawn at the store. I want to draw my own." The pot shows an interesting use of Pattern Darning. The space is well filled. She added the stars at the end.

of their own work. It is a stage when they can become inhibited; they are apt to think that in order to be successful, a stitchery would have to reproduce realistically what they had in mind. For instance, 9-year-olds rarely produce stitcheries with people the way the 6- and 7-year-olds so casually do, because they think the stitchery people would not look true to life. The teacher might explain that if a piece were literal, photographically exact, it would be boring because it would leave nothing to the imagination. They should aim at spontaneous expression of the way they feel about what they see; the interpretation of their idea and a good use of space are what is important.

Nine-year-olds are often fascinated by the precision of stitches, showing an interest in textures and patterns created by one stitch, repeating it to perfection, and glowing in their own proficiency. Pattern Darning and Couching are 9-year-old favorites. They will enjoy looking up detailed stitch diagrams. A book with descriptions and illustrations of stitches should be available to them for consultation. They like to "collect" stitches, to make a list of the stitches they know, and are eager to learn new stitches to add to their list. They will be interested in the relationship between stitches; how a curved stitch becomes a looped stitch, how closing the loop creates a chain, and tightening the chain makes a knot!

Strong motivation will help the 9- and 10-year-olds in acquiring confidence in their ability to give concrete form to an idea. Once they are motivated, they usually plan their stitchery with care and are skillful in details. They want to know how and have a good capacity for working independently.

At that age, if they have experienced creating with stitches, they can become technically just as proficient as the children who were taught stitches academically, with the added advantage of being able to use stitches freely for self-expression.

Fourth Grade Stitchery

At Ravenna School in Seattle, the fourth-grade children were delighted with the idea of stitcheries. Two approaches were tried.

In Nora Erickson's class, motivation was furnished by a study of the State of Washington. Correlating art to geography, the children each made a stitchery map, experimenting on their own, "inventing" as they went along. Variations in terrain and climate offered an opportunity for creative interpretation. The maps were very interesting. (See Color Page 43, C-23.)

In Katherine Aston's class, each child was left free to make a stitchery of his favorite interest. A guest stitchery teacher, Elva Holland, mother of one of the children, demonstrated the mechanics of a few stitches on the blackboard. She then passed around pieces of light-weight white cardboard on which she had worked basic stitches in bright colors of cotton rug yarn. The children could handle these cardboards, turn them around and consult them as much as they wanted. This is a very good teaching aid, well worth the time taken in preparation.

The children proceeded with great enthusiasm, first learning stitches on a small piece of burlap. They discussed what could be achieved with stitches, how they could use them to express textures, and were encouraged to "invent" their own variations. Each one, thinking about the subject of his stitchery, tried to visualize it in his mind, drawing a minimum of lines, if any, on the cloth, working out details freehand, truly creating with stitches and letting the cloth and yarns "speak" to him. (See Color Page 39, C-14.)

Mike likes to go fishing. He pictures his dream: three fish wiggling at the end of the line. An interesting pattern is created by freehand Couching to represent the water. In color, the piece has quite a Van Gogh quality.

On a recent trip to the Smithsonian Institution in Washington, D.C., Chuck H. saw a life size model of a Blue Whale. The stitchery shows a concern for perfection of stitches. The back of the piece is as neat as the front. Chuck used his three favorite stitches: Whipped Running in two shades of green of equal value, outlining the whale; a relaxed Threaded Running to express the seaweed at the left; and Couching for the bottom of the sea and the under part of the whale.

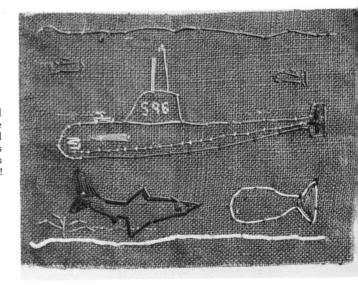

Bruce knew exactly what he wanted to do. He had been working on model submarines at home. He didn't have to draw anything first and went ahead freehand, changing colors often. Couching is his favorite stitch. The least of Bruce's concern was the back of his stitchery. It is definitely uninhibited!

Color Illustrations

C-13. It all started at home with the idea of making a record of stitches learned, using green and different values of pink threads. Soon, however, 10-year-old Theresa's independent and artistic spirit drifted to her favorite subject of the moment — mushrooms! She dyed white cloth a variety of pink values from dark to light to match the shade of her threads. She then proceeded to cut out mushroom shapes and appliquéd them spontaneously, gaily filling the space. Don't miss the T for Theresa! The hem is Eskimo Edge Stitch. (See *The Stitches of Creative Embroidery*.)

C-14. Robin, a gifted, quick and imaginative little girl was obviously fascinated by the medium and tossed off several pieces in rapid succession at school, and at home on her own. "A garden seen by a bird" was worked at home entirely freehand with no drawing either on paper or on the cloth, inventing and composing as she went along. She was creating with stitches in the true sense of the word. (See Fourth Grade, page 36.)

C-15. This was Eileen's first creative stitchery. It was worked freehand directly on green burlap stretched on a light frame, 12-by-16 inches. Eileen wanted to stitch a cat but was unsure as to how to begin. It was suggested that she lay the wine-colored yarn she had chosen on the stretched burlap, coaxing it into a satisfactory cat shape. After this was done, the yarn was held in place by an occasional straight pin and couched down. This line was emphasized by a row of Chain Stitches in variegated pink yarn. The piece is pleasing; it shows spontaneity and a good use of space.

C-16. Although she lives in Seattle, Pamela found the inspiration for her stitchery in a color photograph of a cheetah which was part of a children's store display in Virginia. She added a great deal to it. Her class had been studying ancient Egypt and the cheetah's collar reflects this. Feeling that something was lacking, Pamela was encouraged to try livening the spots with little snips of thread. She did this with great success, using Seed Stitches. The work of an 11-year-old can be just as good as an adult's. (Photograph by Colonel Martin D. McAllister.)

C-13. Theresa P., age 10.

C-14. Robin, age 9.

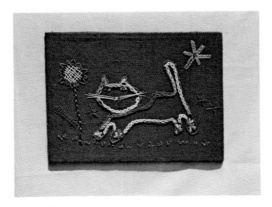

C-15. Eileen, age 9.

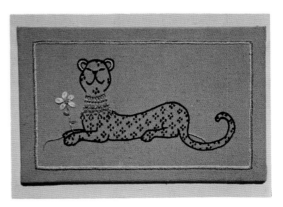

C-16. Pamela, age 11.

Chuck G. is in the fifth grade at Viewlands School in Seattle. His first stitchery was thought out very carefully. He outlined the beetle with close Running Stitches in black wool, then filled the shape with precise stitches in red wool, over one, under one, using a curved needle. Chuck worked during two class sessions and spare time, a quick worker. He infused his beetle with real personality.

At John Rogers School in Seattle, the children in Gladys Turbutt's fifth-grade class were studying the history of pioneers. As an art project, the teacher gave each child a piece of burlap, telling them they could make anything they wished. "Sacajawea with Lewis and Clark" was Theresa's contribution, worked from her own small pencil sketch on paper, then freehand on the burlap, inventing as she went along. At the time Theresa's hair was braided so she braided Sacajawea's hair, braiding it detached from the cloth so that it hung free. Lewis and Clark's caps were made of scraps from discarded fur-lined gloves.

TEN AND ELEVEN YEARS OLD

Like the 9-year-olds, 10- and 11-year-olds love to invent and "collect" stitches. They can work almost any stitch they want to and can work independently. A book with exact diagrams should be available so that they can consult it, find new ideas on how to vary stitches, and devise the best way to obtain the effect they have in mind. By now their tool is becoming easy to manage. Such stitches as the Spider Web variations and stitches with third dimension delight them. They also enjoy filling shapes with textures created by one stitch repeated at even intervals, like Chuck's red beetle.

The 10- and 11-year-olds are good at correlating stitcheries to other subjects. They work well together on class murals; the best ones I have seen came from fifth graders. It is particularly important to create an atmosphere that will stimulate them to research what they are interested in. Theresa's "Lewis and Clark," and the boy's kites shown on Color Page 42, are typical interests at that stage and show pertinent detail. Girls around that age often

(Continued on page 44.)

Color Illustrations

Page 42. Page 43.

C-17. Jeff said he figured nobody would be stitching an ant and he wanted to do something different. His ant has great personality. He did most of the work in three or four days at odd moments at school. He first outlined the body, worked the head and legs. He started to fill the body with red wool in regular Satin Stitch. After a few stitches he decided that he was using too much yarn and would run out of it, so he said: "I figured out how to keep the red yarn on the front." He "invented" a Surface Satin Stitch to fill his need, a good example of the effective result of Jeff's inventiveness and creativity. He added, "I used the Outline Stitch for the grass he was walking in; the earth is under his feet." Most adults would have put the grass under the ant's feet. Putting the grass above shows real thinking and how well the boy identified himself with the ant. Variegated green makes the grass lively; the few horizontal Straight Stitches in brown wool were all that was needed to express earth. (See Fifth Grade, page 44.)

C-18. The main part of Howard's jellyfish is worked in almost fluorescent red wool Satin Stitches, with gold separations. The tentacles are all freely Couched in yarns of different textures and colors. The effect is quite shimmery. Howard was very disappointed when, thumbing through the class copy of *The Stitches of Creative Embroidery,* he found that the Couched Stitch he thought he had invented was a regular named stitch! However, the free Couching is really his own idea. (See Sixth Grade, page 49.)

C-19. FLYING KITES by fifth-grade boys. (See description, page 138.)

C-20. As a neighborhood summer project the girls made the Mexican Quechquemetl they are wearing.

C-21. Kathy has no academic knowledge of the elements and principles of design, yet in her own 9-year-old way she has experienced every one of them. She has to a remarkable degree the ability to let herself be taken over by the feeling she wants to express and letting it flow through her fingers. For instance, having learned the Feather Stitch, no book could have taught her the unique circular expression of it she evolved on the left plant. This "happened" for a number of reasons: spring in the type of yarn used, the child's genuine uninhibited response, and the subtle intuition which led her to work WITH the materials at hand, letting the yarn express what was natural to it, on the material taut over a frame.

When Kathy's freehand design was finished, her teacher at the Needlecraft Shop in Sherman Oaks, California, asked her why she had put in a piggy instead of a butterfly or another bug, or something more related to the caterpillar. (I wondered the same thing myself!) "Kathy, why a piggy?" Came the quick reply from a puzzled child: "Why not?" Indeed Kathy, why not! Adult minds have odd limitations.

C-22. Claire made an original use of Looped Alternating Stem Stitch for her bird. I was fascinated by her effective Pattern Darning in light cream wool on dark green burlap, with a deep gold Back Stitch worked diagonally over each empty space. (See High School, page 50.)

C-23. On her map of the state of Washington, Sherry used Pattern Darning effectively, picking up just one thread of burlap. (See Fourth Grade, page 36.)

C-24. In Jeannette Pruschansky's class, Bryant School, Seattle, Wayne, 11, made this imaginative rooster for a knitting bag as a Christmas present for his mother. Feather Stitch seems particularly appropriate for a rooster! The attractive handle is made of square knots. (See *Macramé* by Virginia Harvey.)

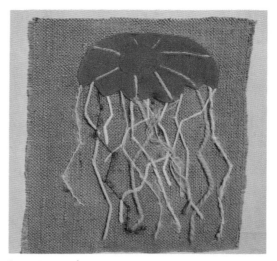

C-17. Jeff, age 10.

C-18. Howard, age 11.

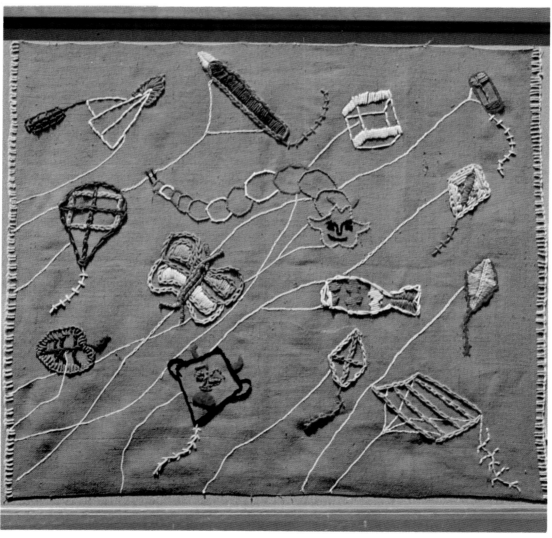

C-19. FLYING KITES, by fifth-grade boys.

C-20. Christine 8, Martha 10, Lisa 6, Susan 8.

C-21. Kathy, age 9.

C-22. Claire, age 17.

C-23. Sherry, age 9.

C-24. Wayne, age 11.

Marilyn is crazy about horses, which is not unusual for an 11-year-old girl. Quoting her teacher, Nora Steen: "She does not own a horse but has often cared for and ridden the neighbor's horse. In addition she reads EVERY horse book she can lay her hands on. She has to be discouraged from using a horse as a model for EVERY art project we try." The outline of this head of a horse — she has worked several — was worked freehand with Couched brown wool. Couching is a good stitch to use for freehand work. The eye is made of brown Satin Stitches with a black Outline Stitch. The free mane adds a great deal to the piece. Long loops of black wool were appropriately clipped, suggesting a firsthand knowledge of horses, great feeling, and intense motivation.

become enamored of horses. Many of them will make a stitchery of a horse and the result is often excellent because the feeling that went in it was strong.

Ten- and 11-year-olds are not quite as interested in the doing as in the finished piece and they want the result to be good; if it is not, they become discouraged. It is therefore important to provide them with suitable materials, although it is amazing to see what they can turn out even with poor quality burlap!

The importance of good craftsmanship should be explained now, if this was not done earlier. Suggestions made in Chapter III, "Designing Stitcheries," become increasingly significant at this stage, helping them to create directly on the cloth.

At home, the idea of a "stitching club" might prove more fruitful than working alone. One way to achieve this is to spark one enthusiastic child who will act as a magnet to draw others into group work. Ten-year-olds are not as self-conscious as 9-year-olds. They like to do things with their families. Stitching a family vacation map or a mural is a good project for this age group.

Fifth Grade Stitcheries (Viewlands School, Seattle, Washington)
(See Frontispiece and Color Page 42, C-17, 18, 19.)

Clarice Ryan is a stimulating teacher whose success is due to the enthusiasm she brings into each subject. She usually has a stitchery of her own going and knows firsthand what can be accomplished with stitches.

One rainy January recess she gave each one of her 30 pupils a small piece of natural color burlap, suggesting that they pull out a thread and reweave

Carla's Teddy Bear, shown in color on the frontispiece. Carla thought that her little sister's brown Teddy Bear would be a good shape for a stitchery. She planned it on paper and drew the outline on burlap. She commented that "brown didn't seem like an exciting color," so she chose variegated pink instead. This was a happy decision. The changes in value add a great deal to the interest. The bear was first outlined in plain pink wool, using Outline Stitch.

To fill the shape with variegated pink, Carla used a stitch which she described as "sort of half Chain and half Feather Stitch." Instead of working it the conventional way towards herself, she worked away from herself with a curved needle. In the center she couched a piece of brown roving, using some of the same roving to frame the whole piece, couching it with brown cotton yarn, a wise choice. Had she couched the brown roving edge with pink yarn, it would have been distracting, while couching the brown tummy with pink tied it in to the rest of the bear. The paws are filled with long brown Buttonhole, the inside of the ears with very pale pink Chain, the center of the eyes and the nose in black, a few red stitches for the mouth. Said Carla: "I added the white pillow because he looked funny sitting by himself on nothing. It makes sort of a background." (Viewlands School, Seattle.)

Donald is crazy about dinosaurs. Said he: "I thought I'd like to stitch one that swims so I made a Plesiosaur." He drew the outline, which he stitched in relaxed Chain Stitches, his thin red yarn doubled. The body is filled with Herringbone, first royal blue, then a lighter blue, and Satin Stitches are used in the flippers. The eye is a green knot. This free Herringbone with heavy cotton yarn "gives sort of a plesiosaury feeling, don't you think so?" said Donald. I couldn't agree more. He was very proud of his neat edge, "five close Blanket Stitches, then one longer one."

David's bold beetle was worked freehand except for the legs and feelers which he drew with a crayon "to be sure they'd come out right." He used heavy cotton rug yarn, outlining the shape with Chain. David said he had to invent a stitch for the filling: "I tried Satin Stitch but too much thread was wasted on the back and I didn't have much thread, so I figured out how I could keep it on the front." This turned out to be the Flat Stitch worked horizontally — quite effective! For the head, his orange Woven Spider Web Stitch is very well done. It was his first attempt.

Brian said: "A Halloween spook card that cost me five cents, the kind you paste on windows, gave me the idea. I tried to make my black widow spiders look real spooky. At the top there is a little web and it has a fly in it. The spiders are weaving a web and there is a little spider there. The tails are extra to make them more interesting."

Doug used a thin black yarn Chain Stitch for the outline of his ladybug. He filled the body with heavy, pink Chain Stitch, the head with red Chain and the lower back with blue Surface Satin. The legs were worked freehand in Running Stitch. Doug said: "The ladybug is running away because a whole bunch of ants are attacking him. I just showed three ants and they are going to win. One has just hooked on."

with a color. Quoting Mrs. Ryan: "They were hooked! After a few minutes everyone wanted to work on a definite stitchery project which would give them an opportunity to discover the technique of stitches as they went along. As they waited impatiently for our order of burlap, designs were drawn on paper, then discussed. The children repeated their drawing freehand on the burlap. We then talked about what stitches could do for the design. They learned and 'invented' many stitches as need arose, making use of large stitch diagrams of basic stitches and referring to the class copy of *The Stitches of Creative Embroidery*. After two or three class sessions, the work was well under way and the children used it as pick-up work in free moments, especially on rainy lunch recesses. They were so enthusiastic that at times they worked hiding behind their desks instead of studying!"

ELEVEN AND TWELVE YEARS OLD

As children reach adolescence, they begin to look at their work with adult eyes; they become increasingly critical and continue to need encouragement. From about the age of 10, they have been gradually loosing the spontaneous, fresh quality of childhood; now, their maturing reasoning powers and their growing critical faculties may unconsciously lead them out of creative expression. Again like the 10-year-olds, they are less interested in the process

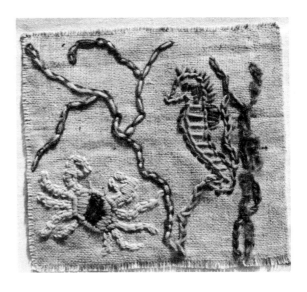

California flowers by 11-year-old Kelly. (Sherman Oaks, California.)

of doing than in the finished product, a factor that will increase as they become older.

At this transitional age, it is more important than ever to stimulate their imagination and help them to give a physical expression, such as drawing, painting, or stitching, to what their imagination has conceived. Stitchery is a particularly good medium for retaining and developing the uninhibited approach of earlier years, for leading them away from realistic representation. Try to develop awareness of design, not as a theory, but as a tactile as well as a visual feeling for textiles and threads. Introduce them to abstract design, suggest that they use nature as a source for design ideas.

The attention span of 11- and 12-year-olds is such that they can accomplish more at one sitting, with quicker results. Their hands are more obedient to the dictates of their minds; given a book with precise directions, there is hardly a stitch they cannot master. Their technique is often amazingly good. If it has flowed from a need, rather than being imposed before there was a need, the result will not only show proficiency, it will also be supple, inventive, and it will express an idea felt.

Sixth Grade Stitcheries (Stevenson School, Bellevue, Washington)

The boys in Nora Steen's class felt rather shy about launching into stitchery. Eleven- and 12-year-olds are at the top of their elementary school: they

April worked directly on the burlap. She sketched the crab lightly and outlined the sea horse with crayon. The seaweed was expressed freely as she stitched along, filling the space between and around the crab and sea horse. The seaweed to the left is a loose Chain Stitch in dark olive green. Inside the chains there is a Running Stitch in light green and dull gold mohair. This is effective and expresses well the feeling of floating seaweed. The other seaweed to the right is worked in Chains of varied greens with one side of the Chain lightly whipped with another shade of green. The use of fuzzy yarn enhances the loosely moving effect. The legs of the crab are outlined with a flat Surface Darning Stitch, picking up just one thread; they are filled with a heavy, closely worked Satin Stitch which by contrast gives a round, heavy feeling well suited to the crab. The body is outlined and filled with heavy Satin Stitches. The sea horse is outlined with Surface Darning, part of it Whipped. Blanket Stitch was worked freehand for the body, Straight stitches for the mane.

The center of Noralie's freehand stitchery is a moon snail shell inhabited by a hermit crab. As often happens, other things had attached themselves and were growing on the shell. The top center is a sea anemone surrounded with sea worms and seaweed. Her hermit crab is really moving along with a good use of Long-Stemmed French Knots. Noralie has an interesting free-form treatment for the seaweed. On the right side, it is particularly effective — free, spontaneous, and airy. A quick Surface Darning Stitch outlines the weeds, picking up just a thread of the turquoise burlap with a sweeping upward motion. The yarn is a mixture of light olive and dull gold. Once the shape was outlined, the inside was filled from side to side with Surface Satin Stitch, which makes it light.

Learning stitches on a small piece of burlap in Nora Steen's sixth grade class. The four on the left side were made by girls, the four on the right side by boys.

Ken, Germany. A mythical God on top of a mountain. "The gate is to keep other people out; just the gods went beyond."

wouldn't want to lose status as he men! Stitchery was a new idea. They were not exactly opposed but wanted to proceed with caution. They were quick to notice that although most of the available pieces of burlap were 12 by 13 inches, there were a few smaller pieces, 8 by 12. They snatched those quickly, figuring that it would involve less work. But they were soon caught in the magic of stitches and all wanted larger pieces for their second and third stitcheries; they couldn't get enough of it.

Each child experimented with stitches on a doodling cloth, learning in about two sessions the Running Stitch, which often turned into Surface Darning, the Back Stitch, Satin, Cross, Blanket, Feather, Chain with personal variations, French Knot, and Couching. After this they were on their own and worked mainly in their spare time.

David, the Berlin Wall. A very moving piece.

Bobby. This stitchery of Switzerland is interesting because of the way it grew. It was all worked free-hand with no drawing — first the cabin in the foreground, next the mountain. "I laid the outline with yarn on the cloth and tacked it down. Then I thought of sheep and grass. It looked too straight up and down, so I put in the storage house on the left, tacking down the long Satin Stitches in a pattern."

The class was studying Sea Life as part of its Science unit. The students had had a field trip to the seashore and were intrigued by what they saw. They looked up many illustrated books. Nora Steen suggested that out of their study they might like to create stitchery pictures as an art project, using their imagination. They all agreed that sea animals and plants would lend themselves to yarns, colors, and stitches. After the initial shock to the boys, all were very enthusiastic. A few drew their ideas on paper first. Most of them launched right into the stitchery with no preliminary drawing, their picture firmly planned in their minds, which gives their stitcheries a free and spontaneous feeling. (See Color Page 42, C-18.)

Another sixth-grade class of Nora Steen's made stitcheries to illustrate their social studies of "Germany and four neighboring countries." Nearly all were worked out on natural burlap with no preliminary drawing or merely a minimal outline of the main feature. These children showed a remarkable use of stitches, first practiced on a small piece of burlap. All were delighted with the experience and learned a great deal.

JUNIOR HIGH SCHOOL

At Meany Junior High School in Seattle, the art teacher, Dorothea Hall, introduced her pupils to stitchery design by suggesting that they cut shapes, any shapes they liked, out of paper, and place them on a sheet of paper the size of the planned stitchery. James, one of the students said: "We arranged the shapes until we got a good effect, then we placed them in the same order on our piece of burlap and chalked around the patterns. We first learned different stitches. Then we outlined the shapes, filling them and parts of the background with stitches. For a difference in texture, I appliquéd three pieces of blue cloth. For stitching I chose colors I like, light and dark blue,

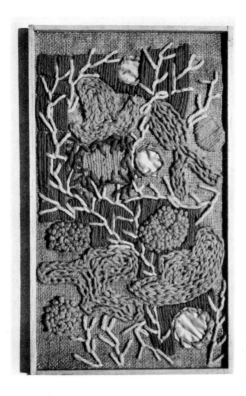

Sara, who lives in Olympia, Washington, worked at home on a quilt made up of individual squares. For each one she chose a subject with a personal meaning. Sara said: "It's a doll like the ones I imagine girls had years ago. She has a poke bonnet deal with flowers on her head. The loops around the neck are the strings of her bonnet."

It is interesting to see how James' Chinese ancestry shows through in his stitchery. (Meany Junior High School, Seattle.)

orange and purple. The last thing was to sort of tie it together with Feather Stitch. It is fun to just design with no thought of anything special. All the kids liked doing it." The students made their own frames with balsa wood glued together at the corners.

HIGH SCHOOL

At Holy Names Academy in Seattle, in one of Sister Joanne Mary's art classes, a stitchery project was to design and decorate three-dimensional birds. For the first step, each student was to construct her own bird with heavy paper, later using the different parts as patterns to trace outlines on cloth. The individual parts were decorated with stitches, then sewn together and stuffed. The result was a variety of imaginative birds. (See Claire's bird, Color Page 43, C-22.)

In another class, after learning stitches on a personal sampler, the students were left free to choose their stitchery subject. The results showed how quickly they can be inspired to develop their own original way of becoming creative with stitches.

Today, many educators are aware and eager to use stitchery as a means of expression contributing to the growth of the child — and of adults too! Artists like Nik Krevitsky, David B. Van Dommelen, teachers like William Cahill Johnson, and many others, because they are men, have helped immeasurably in showing how stitchery is proving to be a stimulating, truly creative outlet for boys as well as girls. A good way to inspire students is to show them the works of stitchery artists, such as Mariska Karasz. They should begin to see how stitches and materials are used to interpret ideas, to create textures. Help them to become aware of design around them and to organize and use their own ideas.

Above, left. Owl by Diane. Above, right. Carlene embroidered, at home, the head scarf she is wearing. (Holy Names Academy.)

Renée's two-dimensional bird shows an interesting use of stitches. (Holy Names Academy.)

Kay's fish mural is well designed. Don't overlook the delightful crab at the bottom! (Holy Names Academy.)

Quails are a familiar sight around Tina's home. She has closely observed the birds and taken in their design possibilities. The quails, on fabrics of different colors, are beautifully decorated with stitches emphasizing their contour. They were individually appliquéd on burlap, over a light padding to give them relief. (Inglemoor High School, Bothell, Washington.)

Left:
Jennifer and David are the grandchildren of the famous artist, Mariska Karasz. Both children are using yarns selected from their grandmother's vast collection. Jennifer's non-objective stitchery is in her grandmother's tradition. David is starting on a stitchery of a bald eagle, his great interest of the moment. He is referring to illustrations in the book under his knee. (Photograph by Colonel Martin D. McAllister.)

II. Learning Stitches

DESCRIPTION OF STITCHES AND VARIATIONS

For their first stitcheries children need to know very few stitches. The first stitches should be discovered as the result of a need, such as the Running Stitch and the Darning Stitch to outline a shape or express a feeling. The need for a more continuous line leads to Double Running; Threaded Running Stitch satisfies the need for a heavier line, and so on.

As children experience the pleasure of discovery, of what repetition or a combination of stitches can do, their feelings can flow from within, their creative ability is given a chance to develop. If they have a specific need, experiment together on how this need could be met, working out two or three possibilities, stressing that there might be other ways waiting to be discovered. The same stitch can express something different just by a change in size, or the weight, color, or texture of yarns.

When children become older and show an interest in the mechanics of stitches, encourage them to broaden their knowledge by following diagrams in the book. Learning new stitches and using them for creative expression is a source of real satisfaction.

Turtle worked by the author to illustrate the Running Stitch.

This was a real effort for 6-year-old Todd. Working a few stitches each day, he outlined in Running Stitches the rockets he had drawn and colored on paper, over which crinoline was stapled.

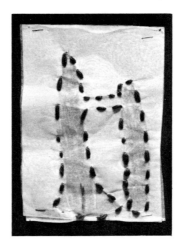

THE FLAT STITCH FAMILY

This is the largest family of stitches, with easy stitches used to follow lines and to fill shapes.

RUNNING STITCH

The name describes the stitch; the needle and thread run in and out of the material. For the first attempt with stitches, a loose heavy weave material such as good quality burlap or two-over-two monk's cloth makes the work easier. Medium-heavy cotton yarns such as lightweight rug yarn, pearl cotton, size 3, which is silky looking, or mat cotton thread of similar weight are easiest to manage.

Work from right to left. Start with a knot on the back at A (Figure 1). Take one stitch at a time, with fairly even intervals, over and under. The stitches should be relaxed or the cloth will pucker. If a stitch looks tight, slide the needle under it and ease it.

The Running Stitch can follow any line you want. It can be straight, curved, even zigzag. If you need a straight line, you can pull out a thread or

1

A

Small, careful stitches outlined 6-year-old Susan's precise drawing over which crinoline was stapled. She used neat Satin Stitches for the yoke of the dress and the red apples in the tree.

crease the material. You can also draw a light line with chalk. Several similar rows together make interesting patterns (Figure 2). You can vary the size of the stitches and use different combinations of sizes (Figure 3), like the long and short notes of a song. The Running Stitch can be used as an outline or to fill shapes. The turtle on page 52 is filled with Running Stitches following the shapes.

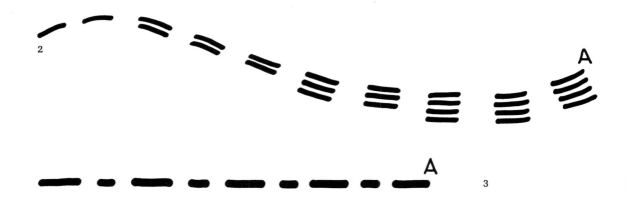

CHECKERBOARD RUNNING STITCH

Under a first row of Running Stitches, work stitches checkerboard fashion, with the second row of stitches under the spaces of the previous row. The third row repeats the first row. Start at A (Figure 4), working from right to left. When you reach the end of a row at B, turn your work around and work back again at C from right to left. See how Virginia Tiffany used this stitch effectively in several places.

BIRDS by artist Virginia Tiffany. (Courtesy of Mrs. Jackson Tiffany, Madison, Wisconsin.)

4

DOUBLE RUNNING STITCH (Holbein)

The Double Running Stitch is useful for a solid line. After working a row of regular Running Stitches from right to left, starting at A (Figure 5), turn your work around at the end of the row and stitch back, starting at a, inserting the needle in exactly the same holes as in the first row but this time filling in

Nancy W., age 6, used Double Running Stitch to outline and fill the flowers she stitched beautifully on a piece of burlap. The idea for the design and for the stitch came from a 2,000-year-old piece of Peruvian embroidery now in the Textile Museum in Washington, D.C. Said Nancy: "I loved the flowers and the colors. It was hard but I'm happy I stuck to it." Her mother mounted the piece as a front pocket on a tote bag.

5

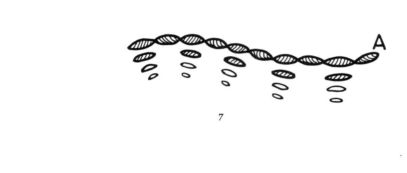

6

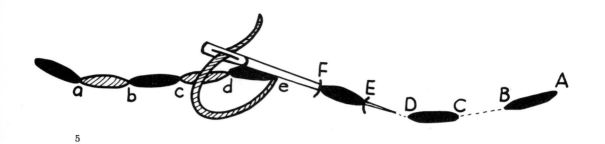

7

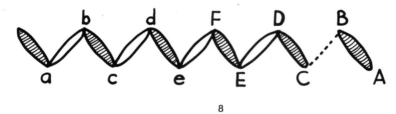

8

9

10

56

the gaps. Try using a different color for the return trip. Several rows with two colors make interesting patterns, especially if they are staggered (Figure 6). This is easy if the material you are working on has a definite weave like burlap or monk's cloth. The Double Running Stitch is one way to fill a shape. It can be worked freely following lines (Figure 7), or it can zigzag (Figures 8, 9).

In Figure 10, after the return trip, another row of Running Stitches was worked over the first row, in the same holes, making the line double in places, giving texture to express growth.

DARNING STITCH

When you pick up very little material between stitches instead of even amounts equal to the stitch, the Running Stitch becomes the Darning Stitch. Used to follow a line or as an outline, it can give a feeling of speed, more so than the Running Stitch. Work from right to left, starting at A (Figure 11). The stitches can vary in length. Figure 12, starting at A, shows a long step and two short steps, followed by a long step and one short step. It can also be used zigzagging (Figure 13).

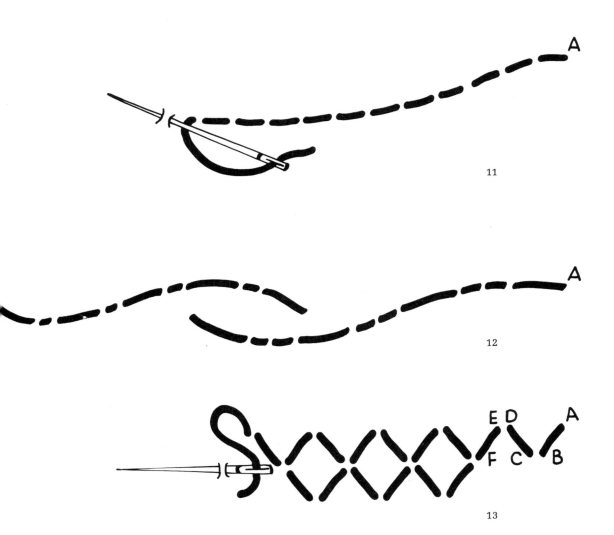

11

12

13

57

Rocky, age 11, with Holland in mind, started his piece by outlining the edge with Buttonhole Stitch "to sort of think about what I would do." He sketched the outline of the windmill very lightly, working the details freehand, also the flowers and the cloud. The workmanship is remarkable. When he was through, Rocky felt that the sky needed something at the top so he started a row of light blue yarn, "over four, under two," following the weave of the burlap. For the second row, he accidentally went one stitch farther and soon realized that he was creating a pattern. This was intriguing. After five rows, he reversed the direction to see what would happen. Because he was alert, Rocky was able to make good use of what had happened. He experienced Pattern Darning.

PATTERN DARNING

Rows of Darning Stitch can be worked into all sorts of patterns either with stitches of the same length or in various combinations of longs and shorts. For centuries this stitch has been a favorite way of filling a shape because it is economical, since most of the thread stays on the surface of the material. It also produces interesting textures. Three or five rows close together, with no material showing between rows, make an attractive solid outline.

Work from right to left (Figure 14). When you reach B, turn your work around and work from C to D, then E to F, and so on. If you work it with heavy yarns and with a small amount of material showing between rows, it can become a ground cover. Figures 15 and 16 show two ways of expressing movement. Many patterns can be invented (Figures 17, 18). Try changes in texture, a heavy yarn between two rows of lighter yarn (Figure 19).

DETACHED DARNING

An interesting way to fill a shape and to give it extra texture is by means of Darning Stitches worked detached from the base material, going through it at the edges only, weaving back and forth without picking up the ground material. To be worked satisfactorily you should either have a very firm base

B ... A

F ... C ... E ... D

14

15

16

17

18

19

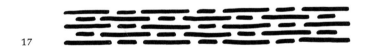

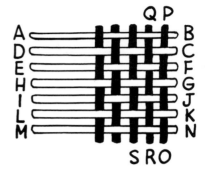

20

THE HOLY FAMILY. A good use of Detached Darning. (Courtesy of Dr. and Mrs. Harold B. Fenech, Detroit, Michigan.)

material, as was the case for the Holy Family hanging, or else use a frame or hoop to keep the material taut.

The possibilities of designs in texture are almost endless. Threads can vary in color, in texture, or in weight. They can be laid horizontally, diagonally, or in a combination of horizontal and diagonal. The laid threads can be close to each other or they can be spaced for a more open effect. It is one way of filling a shape quickly. Try it first with heavy yarns.

Bring the needle and thread out at A (Figure 20), insert at B, out at C, in at D, out at E, and so forth. When you reach the lower edge, insert at N, come out at O. Weave over and under with a rounded-point needle (tapestry), without picking up material, until you reach the farther edge. Keep your woven rows close together — in the illustration they are shown separated only to help you to understand how to work them. Insert at P, come out at Q, close to P. Weave back to the opposite side, reversing the previous row, under and over, to R. Insert and come out at S, repeating the pattern of the first row. It is just like darning socks except that you have material under the darning instead of a hole.

There are many weaving patterns possible. For instance, you can weave over two, under two, or over three, under three, for a checkerboard effect, especially if you change color for the weaving. Detached Darning is a quick way to fill a large shape.

BACK STITCH

The Back Stitch has a crisp texture that is all its own. Instead of running forward, as with the Running Stitch, the Back Stitch takes a step backwards, then forward.

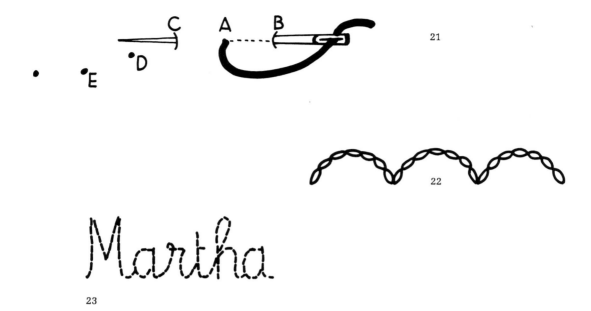

21

22

Martha

23

Work from right to left. Bring the needle and thread out at A (Figure 21), take a stitch backwards to B, coming out at C, in front of A. Go back in at A, in the A hole, then on to D, back to C, in the C hole, and so on.

The Back Stitch is one of the best stitches to use for a sharp outline; it goes around curves easily (Figure 22) which makes it good for writing names (Figure 23). It can be worked into interesting designs. When used as a filling, close rows together give a neat, pebbly effect (Figure 24).

24

SPLIT BACK STITCH

This Split Stitch variation is used in the embroideries of Sweden. It is an easy way to work textured lines, stems of flowers, and the outlines of leaves. It brings variety to the Back Stitch. Work towards you, with a sharp-point needle. Start with a Back Stitch. Bring the needle and thread out at A (Figure 25). Take a step backwards in at B and come out forward at C. But instead of going back to A, insert the needle just a little above A at D, splitting the thread in two. Come out at E. Go back just a little above C, split the thread, going in at F, out at G, and so on. In the conventional Split Stitch, the yarn is split with the needle coming from back to front. This is very difficult to do well. It is easy to split a thread with the needle going in from front to back because you are able to see better what you are doing. If you use two threads in the needle at the same time, the result will look like a Chain Stitch. Split Back Stitch has one disadvantage — it uses a lot of thread.

25

Ceremonial dance sash, South West United States. Both front and back of the sash show the effect obtained by the Back and Running stitch, whether worked on an upright loom or with a needle. (Courtesy of the Smithsonian Institution.)

BACK AND RUNNING

This stitch combination was found on a sash woven by American Zuni Indians. It is an effective way of filling a shape solidly, with a slightly raised rib texture caused by the Back Stitches. Although, in fact, this is a weaving technique with the colored yarns worked in as the weaving proceeds, the result looks as though it had been embroidered. It can be worked just as well with a needle, and it sometimes is. Work it on an even weave material such as two-over-two monk's cloth. Distances have to be worked carefully for the first row, after which the pattern is easy to follow.

26

Bring the needle and thread out at A (Figure 26); take a Back Stitch from A to B, then back to A. Pull through. Insert the needle at C, the length of AC being about one and a half times to twice the length of AB. Come out at D. DC is the same length as AB. Now take a Back Stitch from D to C and back to D. Over to E, under to F, then a Back Stitch from F to E, and back to F. It is a complete Back Stitch followed by a Running Stitch. The Back Stitches stand out and form ribs alternating with flat areas, producing an interesting pattern (Figure 27). You might try a zigzag Back and Running (Figure 28).

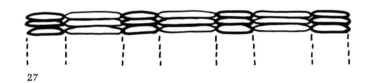

27

28

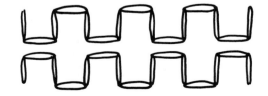

SEED OR DOT STITCH

A Seed or Dot Stitch is made up of two Back Stitches worked in the same holes, AB, AB (Figure 29). It can be worked at random or in patterns, or even overlapping. You will find it effective for plants and seeds (Figure 30). It is often used to fill a shape or a background but can also be used as a line. For a lighter effect, use one Back Stitch instead of two. Try using three for a rounder seed or a flower petal, working the center stitch first, then one on each side. If you are in a hurry, you can double your thread and coax the two threads to lie side by side.

30

Sandpiper worked by the author to illustrate Seed or Dot Stitch.

WHIPPED AND THREADED STITCHES

Stitches can be Whipped, Threaded, or Double Threaded. This is effective for outlines; it also produces interesting textures when several rows are close together. The same thread can be used, or you can try a variety of weights, colors, and textures to produce different effects. It is a good way to use metallic threads.

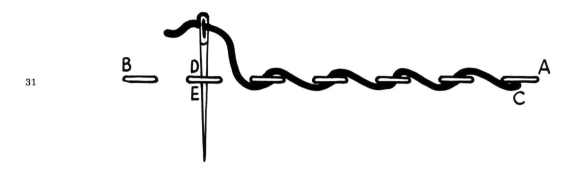

31

WHIPPED STITCHES

Work a row of Running Stitches from right to left as from A to B (Figure 31). Then, using a needle with a rounded point, such as a tapestry needle, whip the stitches, again from right to left. Starting at C, just under the first stitch, go over to the next stitch, pointing the needle from the top downward, "under the bridge" as shown at DE, without picking up any material. As you pull the thread, let it lie relaxed between the first two stitches. Continue to the next stitch, from the top downward, "under the bridge," with the whipping thread neither too tight nor too loose, and end behind the last stitch, at B. The whipping thread goes through the material only at the beginning and at the end.

Once you have mastered whipping a Running or a Darning Stitch, you can use the same method for many stitches: the Double Running, the Back Stitch, rows of Seed or Dot Stitches. When you whip a red Running or Darning Stitch with a white thread of the same weight, the result has a candy cane effect. The outline and the division lines of the turtle, page 52, are Whipped Back Stitch. This gives a definite line with a corded look.

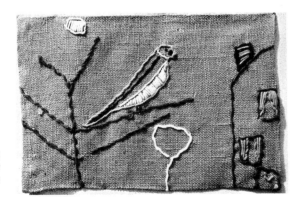

Nancy G.'s first stitchery, at age 8, was worked mainly in Whipped Running Stitch. Notice how the weight of the bird seems to have bent the branch.

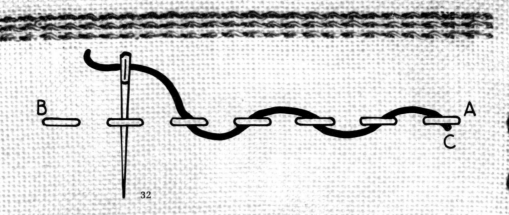

B · · · · · · A
C
32

THREADED STITCHES

Threaded Stitches start the same way that Whipped Stitches do, with a row of Running Stitches from right to left, from A to B (Figure 32). The same yarn or a different one can be used for threading; the result often looks more interesting if a heavier or darker yarn is used.

Start at C, under the first Running Stitch; go under it from below upward, without picking up material. Go under the next stitch, this time from top downward "under the bridge" and continue upward and downward to the end of the line, going through the material to the back under the last stitch at B. The threaded stitches should be relaxed, neither too tight nor too loose. If one looks too tight, slide the needle under and ease it up.

Double Threaded Stitches create some of the most beautiful textured lines you can ever work. Try them with different weights of threads in either the same color or different values of the same color such as light, medium, and dark, or in contrasting colors.

Start with a single threaded line as in Figure 32. When you reach the end, turn your work around and thread back (Figure 33). Threading two or three parallel rows of Running Stitches creates beautiful patterns (Figure 34). Try also two thin threads with a heavy thread (Figure 35). If you want to introduce another color or a different value of the same color, you can work Seed or Running Stitches in the open spaces (Figure 36).

Back Stitches and Seed Stitches can be Threaded and Double Threaded (Figure 37). Threaded Checkerboard Running Stitch makes an interesting design obtained by threading the Checkerboard Running Stitch, back and forth (Figure 38). One of my favorite ways is Double Threading the two rows of Checkerboard Running Stitch from inside out.

Threading can be between horizontal and vertical lines (Figure 39). Try threading the Zigzag Darning Stitch (Figure 40) first ABCDEF, and so on until your last slant stitch, then start to thread at a, going "under the bridge," made by the slanting stitches, alternately downward and upward. Threading can be worked many ways. Try to invent new ways.

Page borders worked by the author to illustrate Whipped and Threaded Stitches.

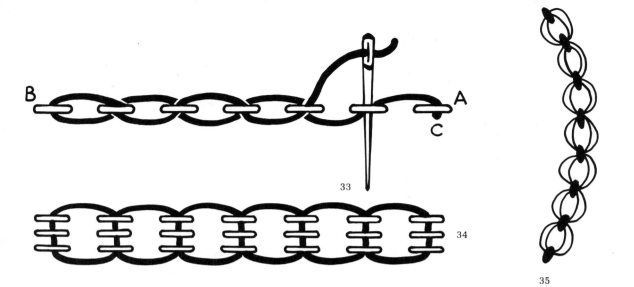

34

36

37

38

39

40

Twelve-year-old Carolyn found an effective way of expressing shimmering water. She worked freehand Threaded Running Stitch, using cotton rug yarn. This gave a feeling of motion to the water. The effect was further enhanced by filling the spaces between with green Seed Stitch at various angles. The hulls of the boats are Couched green yarn for one, red for the other, the sails white Satin Stitch. The seagulls are two grey Straight Stitches and the cloud white Stem Stitch.

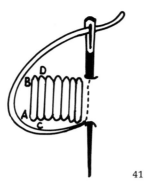

41

SATIN STITCH

The Satin Stitch is made up of Back Stitches worked close together to cover a shape (Figure 41). You will see a great deal of it in the embroideries of the past. Working from left to right, bring the needle and thread out at A, insert at B, come out at C close to A, insert at D, close to B. When the stitches are too long they tend to look untidy. If this happens, one solution is to tie the stitches down the center or in patterns with stitches such as Back, Chain, Feather, and others. Tying down gives you a chance to bring in color variations and texture. Satin Stitch is a difficult stitch to work well. It is also wasteful of thread since there is as much thread on the back as there is on top.

SURFACE SATIN STITCH

Surface Satin Stitch is more practical than regular Satin Stitch because all the thread stays on the surface of the material. There are two ways of working Surface Satin Stitch. One is to pick up a very small amount of material at opposite ends, working from right to left, up and down on the surface of the

Jimmy, age 9, used Surface Satin Stitch for his prim tiger.

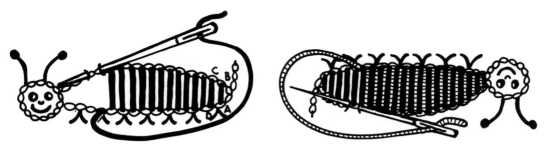

42　　　　　　　　　　　　43

material. The other way, easier and more satisfactory, is to pick up a slightly larger amount of material, leaving a small space between each stitch (Figure 42). When you reach the end, turn the material so that you are still working from right to left and fill in the open spaces (Figure 43). This is what Jeff did for his red ant after he had outlined the shape with Stem Stitches (see Color Page 42, C-17). He started with regular Satin Stitches, then found it wasteful and "invented" Surface Satin Stitch.

It is often difficult to keep even edges when working Satin Stitches. The Hungarians have a neat way of solving the problem by first outlining the shape with small Chain Stitches. Satin or Surface Satin Stitches are worked through the middle of the Chain Stitches, as in Figures 42 and 43. It gives an attractive finished edge to the shape. Another solution is to work a row of Outline or Back Stitches all around the shape.

TWISTED SATIN STITCH

To give a raised textured surface to the Satin Stitch, a second stitch can be twisted around the first stitch. Bring the needle and thread out at A (Figure 44). Insert at B. Come out again at A and pull through. Slide the needle under AB without picking up any material, and pull through gently. Insert the needle at C, a little above B, but not in the same hole, and come out at D for the beginning of the next stitch. These stitches can be worked close together or with spaces between them.

44

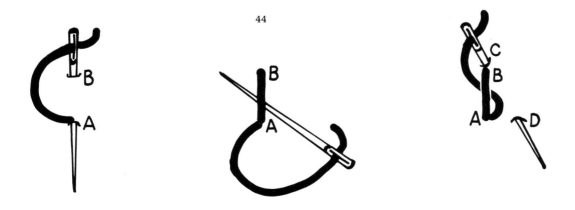

45

B D F H

A C E G

46

BC FG

ADEH

47

B   A   48

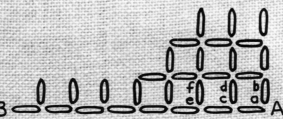

Band of flowers worked by the author to illustrate Straight Stitches.

49

STRAIGHT STITCHES

Straight Stitches are very easy to work. They can be the same or different lengths, going in any direction you want. They can also be worked in rows or in patterns. They should not be too long or else they won't stay in place. If they are too long, tack them down with Back Stitches as was done over pairs of long Straight Stitches in Figure 45.

In working designs with Straight Stitches, the result can be varied by the way the stitches are made. For instance, if you are working the petals of a flower, for a straight effect follow the first diagram (Figure 46). For petals with a curved, relaxed effect, follow the second diagram (Figure 47).

You can make designs more exciting by having two or three yarns threaded together in the same needle, using variations of color or texture: three close values of one color, such as light, medium, and dark threaded together, will make interesting flower petals. If you wanted a daisy type flower, you could thread a bright yellow wool together with a lighter yellow cotton, a finer wool, and perhaps a thread of pale yellow silk, and let the yarns fall where they will.

One way to fill a shape is to work parallel rows of Darning Stitch a short distance from each other, using one color — royal blue, for instance — picking up one thread of the material, from A to B (Figure 48); then with another color — red perhaps — work Straight Stitches at a right angle to the Darning Stitches, ab-cd-ef, or any way you want.

Children often enjoy making stick figures with Straight Stitches (Figure 49).

71

52

51

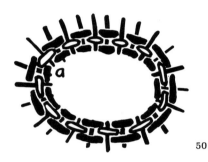

50

WOVEN STRAIGHT STITCHES

Work rings of Straight Stitches to form a base for weaving in and out in the manner of the Spider Web Stitch (Figure 50). An interesting variation is obtained by using two yarns threaded together in a needle, working around a circular, oval, or square base (Figures 51-52).

Lay the double foundation stitches from AB, CD, EF, GH, and so on around. When the foundation is laid, bring the needle and thread out at a. Weave from right to left over one half and under the second half of each foundation stitch. Continue over and under each half of the double Straight Stitches all the way around. The next time around, reverse the procedure used for the first row; instead of over and under, weave under and over each half of the double Straight Stitches. Continue to alternate rows in this way. Weave around as many times as you like, and, if necessary, pick up a small amount of material when the weaving thread does not stay in place. End behind a Straight Stitch. (See last two floral designs on page 70).

THREADED STRAIGHT STITCHES

Threading Straight Stitches is a lot of fun. It leads to many interesting designs, such as growing forms, grasses, fascinating circular shapes, quick and easy flowers. It is one of the easiest ways to inspire children to create spontaneously with stitches: threading is easier than looped stitches.

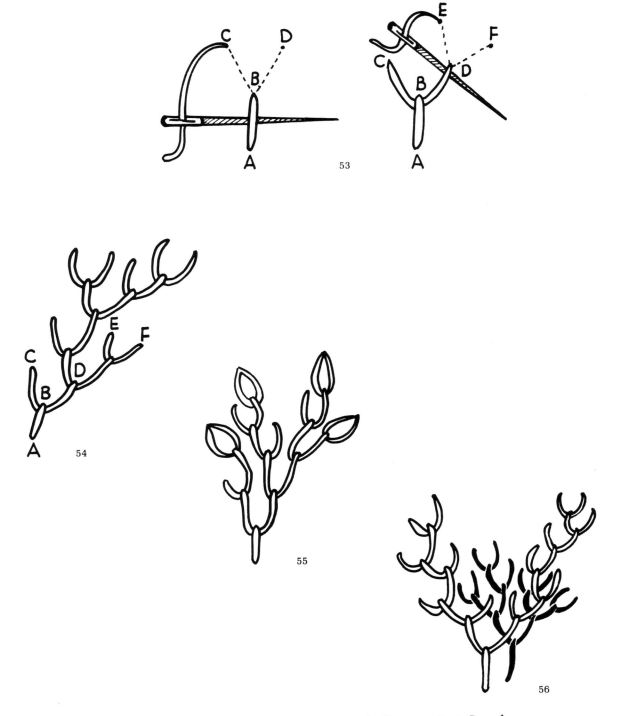

53

54

55

56

Start with a Straight Stitch from A to B (Figure 53). Come out at C and thread under AB, insert at D. Continue threading under either CB or DB. The arms of the threaded stitches can vary in length; they can be stretched out, as in Figure 54, or they can be quite close together. Some can have arms joined together on the ends (Figure 55). How about several plants worked on top of each other with threads of different weights? (Figure 56.)

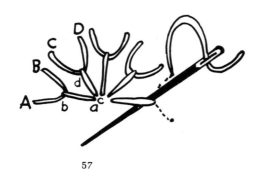

57

59

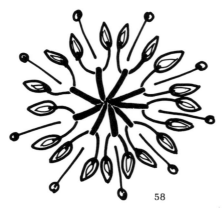

58

Flowers of any size can be made by starting with a center of Straight Stitches, ab, cd (Figure 57), or an Eye Stitch (see page 78). Then bring the needle and thread out at A, thread under the Straight Stitch, ab, without picking up any material; insert at B. Come out at C, thread under the next Straight Stitch and insert at D, and on around. You can make as many rows as you like, threading under the edges of the last outstretched arms, ending the last row with arms outstretched or arms joined (Figure 58). Many stitches can be added effectively: Long Stemmed Knots which look like stamen, or plain French Knots, Seed Stitches, or Detached Chains.

The center of a flower can start with a freehand Eye Stitch, or it can be worked around an open space which can later be filled with French Knots, Seed Stitches, or any kind of filling you choose (Figure 59).

CLOUD FILLING

Another threaded stitch, useful for filling large areas quickly, is Cloud Filling. Heavy yarns will cover an area fast, while sewing threads will give a lacy effect. The distance between the foundation stitches will determine the final effect, whether you want a solid covering or whether you want the background material to show. Foundation and threading stitches can be worked with the same thread, but by using threads of different texture or color the result is more exciting.

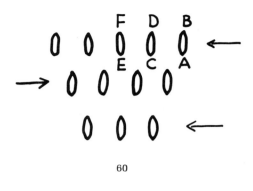

60

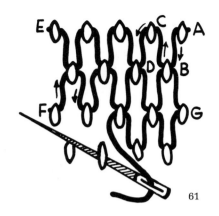

61

First work a foundation of small, spaced, upright stitches from right to left, A to B, over to CD, then EF, to the end of the row (Figure 60). Turn your work around and work a second row, a short distance below with the stitches under the spaces of the first row. At the end of the row, turn your work around; the third row is like the first, the fourth like the second, and so forth.

When the foundation is laid, covering all the shape, start threading. With a round-point tapestry needle, two rows are threaded together, the first with the second, the third with the second, snaking in and out, horizontally. Work from right to left. Bring the needle and thread out at A (Figure 61). Thread under the first upright stitch, then down under B, without catching material. Up under C, down under D, and on to the end of the double row. Go through the material, behind the last foundation stitch, at E; turn your work around and come up at F, at the beginning of the third row, just as you did at A in the first row. Go down under the next stitch in the second row, as you did at B, up and under the next and so on to the end of the row. Insert at G, pass your thread under a stitch at the back to anchor your thread, and come out again at G. Turn your work around and thread the third and fourth rows together as you did the first and second.

With Cloud Filling as a base, you can work many interesting textures. A heavy thread Seed Stitch, a French Knot, a Detached Chain, Cross Stitches, can be added to the open spaces. Another color can be threaded over. Try rows of Back Stitches (Figure 62) over the threaded stitches, or else Zigzag Darning.

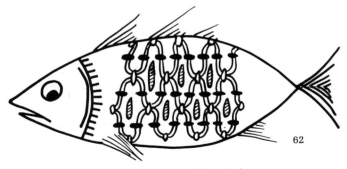

62

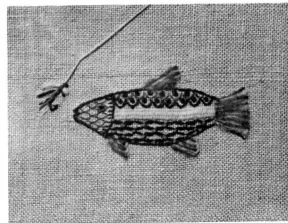

Curt, age 8, had made a successful stitchery at school. Later at home his mother taught him two new stitches. One was Cloud Filling, which fills the lower part of his fish. The other, for the center band, was Cretan Stitch which he found easy, following the burlap weave.

Dragonfly worked by the author to illustrate the Wave Stitch.

WAVE STITCH

The Wave Stitch is another Threaded Stitch with interesting coverage possibilities. It is a quick way to fill a shape and is economical of thread since most of it stays on the surface of the material. Much of the effect depends on the weight of the thread used. It can be worked with heavy wool so as to completely cover the base material; or, by using a light thread and long stitches, you can achieve a lacy effect, a light, airy feeling. It is adaptable and covers any shape easily.

Start with a row of Straight Stitches (Figure 63) or, if you are working a curved area, radiating stitches at the top of the shape you want to cover (Figure 64). For these foundation stitches, working from right to left, bring the needle and thread out at A, go in at B, out at C, in at D, out at E, in at F, and so on. After the last foundation stitch, GH, start the threading. Use a round-end tapestry needle. Turn your work around so as to work again from right to left. From the last stitch, which went in at H, bring the needle and thread out at I. Pass under GH without picking up any material; go in at J and take a very small stitch, JK, thread under the next Straight Stitch, above, in at L, and so on to the end of the row, inserting at M. Turn your

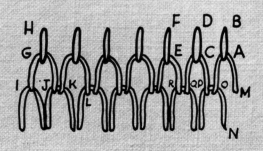

63

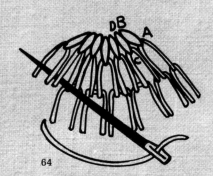

64

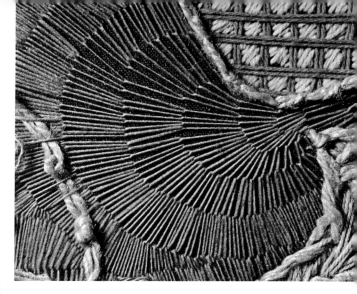

Detail from a stitchery by teacher-artist William Cahill Johnson, showing an interesting use of the Wave Stitch. (Photograph by Fred Figgins.)

Carla's apples show another way of using the Wave Stitch. (See the whole piece, page 134.)

work and bring the needle out at N. At this point, there are two ways of threading: one is the true Wave Stitch, which threads BEHIND the sides of the little picked-up stitches such as OP, QR; the other way, which looks like a knitted surface (Figure 65), threading behind MO, PQ, and so on. You have to decide what effect you want.

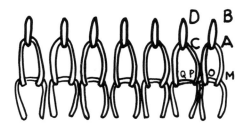

65

This detail from a 19th-century Kantha from India illustrates an effective use of several stitches to fill shapes, including freehand Eye Stitch. (Courtesy of the Cleveland Museum of Art. Gift of the Textile Arts Club.)

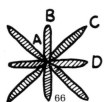

EYE STITCH

When Straight Stitches are worked from a center point in regular geometric patterns, with the outside edge forming a square, they are called Eye Stitches.

Bring the needle and thread out at A in the center, working from back to front (Figure 66). Instead of a knot, leave a length of thread in the back, working it in later over the back of the stitches, A to B, back to A, A to C, and so on around. You can use the same idea, working freehand from the same center, varying the length of the stitches and in any direction. You can change threads and bring in color and texture variations (Figure 67). This can form an interesting base for a Spider Web Stitch (see page 123).

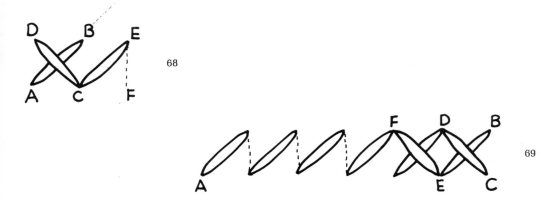

68

69

CROSS STITCH

The traditional Cross Stitch is made with two Straight Stitches of equal size crossing each other diagonally. It is easiest to work on even-weave canvas type material and looks best when all the stitches are crossed in the same direction. They can be worked individually, starting at A (Figure 68), over to B, under to C, and over to D. From D under back to C, over to E, under to F, and so on. They can also be worked in rows (Figure 69), working first from left to right, A to B, then back, crossing the stitches on the return journey, CD-EF, or you can work them first from right to left, whichever is easiest for you.

If you want to fill a shape with Cross Stitch in the traditional way, draw your subject on squared paper and square off the edges of the design, filling it with one Cross Stitch for each square. The people of Scandinavian countries use Cross Stitch very skillfully.

You can cross stitches vertically and horizontally and make Upright Cross Stitch (Figure 70). Figure 71 might be worked into a neat fence, possibly outlined in Back Stitch. Stitches crossed one way or another make good fillings.

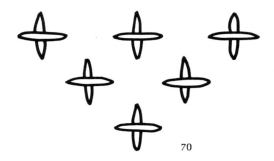

70

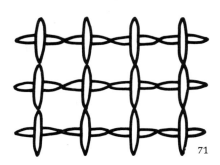

71

DOUBLE CROSS STITCH

Start with a regular Cross Stitch, ABCD. Then on top of it work an Upright Cross Stitch, EFGH (Figure 72). It can be an interesting way of filling a shape, in blocks (Figure 73), or individually, separated, for instance, by rows of other stitches such as Running or Darning, as on the little girl's dress.

An interesting variation is obtained by using different weights of thread or two values of one color, first working the regular Cross Stitch, then changing threads and working the Upright Cross Stitch.

In Figure 74, the Double Cross Stitches are worked freehand. The long Straight Stitches are couched down with rows of Back Stitches. The stamens are Long Stemmed Knots.

72

73

74

Little girl worked by the author to illustrate the Double Cross Stitch.

75

76

STAR STITCH

Work a Double Cross Stitch, then add a third small cross on each side of the vertical stitch (Figure 75). This is useful when the Double Cross Stitch is large and needs anchoring. It also gives the opportunity to add additional colors. Try working freehand Star Stitches or Double Cross Stitches and joining the ends for flower patterns (Figure 76).

OBLONG CROSS STITCH

Work long Cross Stitches vertically or horizontally (Figure 77). Try threading two different weights of yarns in the same needle and work freehand Oblong Cross Stitch. It is a quick, free way to fill a shape — the trunk of a tree, for instance — giving it texture. When you work a Double Oblong Cross Stitch and make the last stitch very small, the result is similar to the Sheaf or Bundle Stitch (Figure 78).

77

78

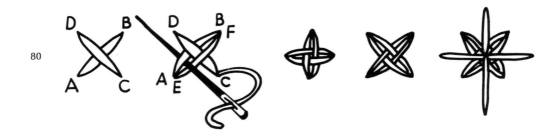

CROSS STITCH FLOWER

The Cross Stitch Flower is very easy to learn, especially if you use heavy threads. It can be worked in rows, or freehand, to fill a shape. It can also be massed to make up flowerets of a composite flower such as lilacs or batchelor buttons (Figure 79). It is best to use heavy thread.

The Cross Stitch Flower is made up of two Cross Stitches on top of each other, in the same holes (Figure 80). Start with a regular Cross Stitch, ABCD. From D, return to A, in the same hole; go over to B (EF), then down to C. On your way back to D, with the point of the needle and without picking up material, go over EF, under AB; or if AB presents itself first, under AB and over EF; the result is basically the same. Pull through and insert at D.

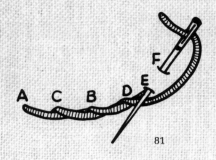

81

82

STEM, CREWEL, AND OUTLINE STITCH

The Stem, Crewel, and Outline Stitch can be used for a line or to outline shapes. Work from left to right. Bring the needle and thread out at A (Figure 81). Holding the thread down with your left thumb, insert the needle at B. With the thread still down, come out at C, half way between A and B. Pull the thread through. Go over and in at D, coming out at B with the thread down. Pull through. Go over to E, coming out at D, and so on. Always bring the needle out in the hole of the stitch you just made and try to make your stitches even in size.

When the thread is kept DOWN, the stitch is called Stem or Crewel. The result is a jagged line. It is called Outline when the thread is kept ABOVE the needle: this gives you a straighter line. Whether the stitch is called Stem, Crewel, or Outline, you should always keep the thread on the same side of the needle, below or above the needle, until the end of the line. Do what comes easiest to you for the effect you like best. Work one or two inches each way to see the difference. The back of your work should look like a neat row of Back Stitches.

The Stem or Outline Stitch can be used as a filling, either with rows close together or with a space between. For circular shapes, start on the outside to preserve a sharp edge; on a sharp curve, keep the thread outside the curve. If you want to fill a square or rectangle, use parallel rows, horizontal or vertical. When you are outlining shapes such as animals, plants, abstract forms, and don't want to fill the whole shape with stitches, try adding one, two, or three rows of small Running Stitches just below the Outline Stitch edge (Figure 82).

Leaves worked by the author to illustrate the Stem Stitch.

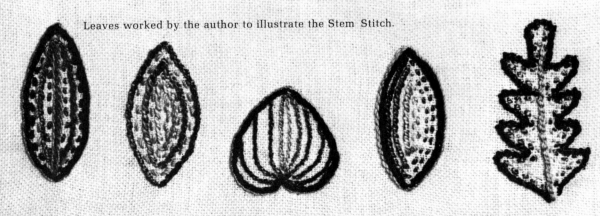

LONG STEM STITCH

An interesting variation of the Stem Stitch is the Long Stem Stitch, worked by picking up a small amount of material instead of going back in the hole of the previous stitch (Figure 83). This leaves most of the yarn on the right side. Rows can be worked close together or spaced to fill a shape quickly. Remember to work with the thread outside a curve; for instance, if you are working a leaf shape, keep the working thread outside the leaf, starting each side from the stem end. On page 134, Carla used the Long Stem Stitch for several of her leaves.

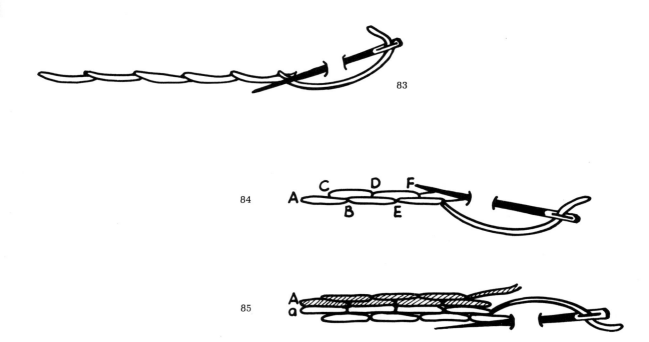

ALTERNATING STEM STITCH

This stitch is worked like the Stem Stitch from left to right. But instead of holding the thread down for every stitch, as in Figure 81, the thread is held alternately down for the first stitch, from A to B, up for the second from C to D, down for the third from B to E, up for the fourth from D to F, and so on (Figure 84).

A beautiful line with many uses is obtained by working two rows close to each other (Figure 85). Start the second row just below the first row at a, reversing the first row, holding the thread up for the first stitch, down for the second, up for the third, and so on. The two rows will look like four rows of stitches. It is a quick way of working a border or the textured outline of a shape. It is particularly effective when worked with heavy threads such as pearl cotton in size 3. Try using two close values of the same color (one darker than the other), for instance, the top row in light gold, the lower row in medium gold.

The goat and flowers were worked by the author to illustrate the possibilities of the Looped Alternating Stem Stitch. A sheep named "Lisa" provided the wool for the goat. (See the back of this stitchery, page 160.)

LOOPED ALTERNATING STEM STITCH

This stitch has been used for centuries by rug makers in many countries, under the name of Ghiordes, Turkish, Rya, or Flossa Knot. It is an Alternating Stem Stitch with one side looped. It gives a third dimension to stitcheries, to furry animals, bird feathers, fish scale, growing plants and flowers. (See Claire's bird, Color Page 43, C-22). A good introduction to it is to practice the Alternating Stem Stitch until the mechanics of the stitch are familiar. You will find it easiest to learn on a coarse-weave material, such as two-over-two monk's cloth, burlap, or canvas. To make it easier to learn, the directions given here are for working on burlap or a fabric of similar weight, with rug yarns, wool or cotton, or pearl cotton, size 3. For other fabrics, the size of the stitches, as from A to B, would be approximately 1/8 inch.

Work from left to right (Figure 86). Bring the needle and thread out at A. Holding the working thread UP, insert at B, two threads of the fabric over, and come out at A, in the A hole. Pull the needle and thread through a little snugly. Now, holding the thread down with your left thumb, insert the needle at C, to the right of B, two threads of the fabric over, and come back out at B.

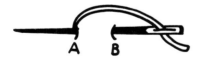

86   continued on next page

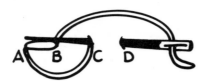

86

continued

This time don't pull the thread completely through but leave a loop. The size of this loop depends on the effect you want. (See note below.) With your left thumb holding the loop down, and your working thread up, insert the needle at D, two threads of the fabric over, and come back out at C. Pull completely through. This upper stitch should always be pulled a little snugly, though not tightly enough to pucker the material. (Remember to hold the loop down.) Continue with the thread down, inserting the needle at E, coming back out at D. Pull partly through, leaving a loop. Holding the loop down and the working thread up, insert at F, coming out at E, with the thread DF snug, and so forth.

Loops need not always be the same size; a variety of sizes can be used, as, for instance, in growing forms. Try working over three threads of the fabric or over one, to see how the effect varies. The stitch can also be worked with the loops up instead of down. For growing forms, you can turn around the end and work back, still from left to right (Figure 87).

After you have learned the stitch straight, on material with a definite weave, work freely in any direction. Work in circles for flowers, with some of the loops cut (Figure 88). Try also several rows close together, one above the other, or facing each other, or back to back (Figure 89). You can overlap the stitches or vary the size, long and short.

Loops can also be cut for a tufted effect or for a fringe. This was the way it was used for the grass in front of the New Hebrides hut, page 142. Areas covered with Looped Alternating Stem Stitch can be cut while others are left uncut for variety in texture. It is a stitch filled with possibilities and children make their own wonderful discoveries.

87

88

89

(NOTE: If you need to have very even loops and find it difficult to maintain the same size, cut a length of cardboard 1/2 inch wide and loop the thread around it, or you can use a pencil or even your little finger inside the loop and snug up the thread around it; you will quickly acquire a feel for size.)

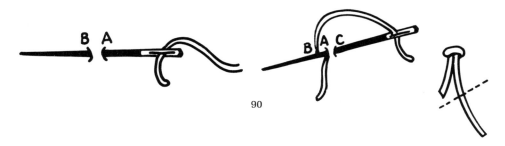

90

FRINGE STITCH

Instead of rows of loops, individual knots can be made, each forming a little fringe. These are easy and amusing to work; they are useful when you need a scattered effect, and they make wonderful cat's whiskers!

If you want a whole row of Fringe Stitches, it is quickest to use the Looped Alternate Stem Stitch and cut it. But for individual fringes, without knotting the end of your working yarn, take a very small stitch from right to left, from A to B (Figure 90). If you are working on burlap, work AB under one thread of the burlap. Pull almost through until you have about an inch of yarn left on top, or whatever length you want. This represents half of your fringe. With the working yarn up, take a stitch from C to A, the same size as AB, and pull through snugly, holding on to the first half of the fringe with your left thumb. Cut the yarn coming from A to match the length of the first half. Start again wherever you want the next fringe to be and repeat exactly what you did from A to B and C.

The fringe can be made going up instead of down. You can also double your yarn for a heavier fringe. Wouldn't it make nice scattered grass? You can make the fringe long and tie down each half with a Back Stitch part way down. The fringe can follow any design you want and I am sure you will invent many uses for it.

FERN STITCH

The Fern Stitch can be used for growing things, ferns, the veins of leaves and petals, also for many designs (Figure 91). It is made up of three Straight Stitches coming from the same point.

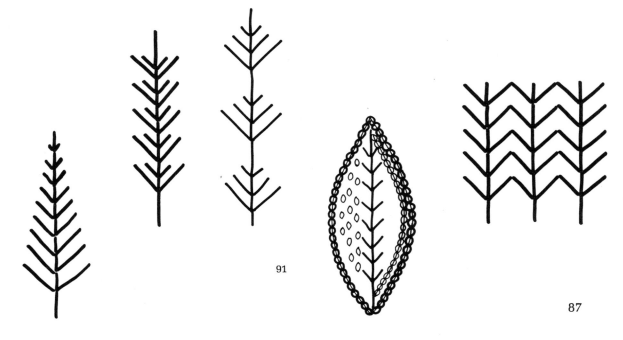

91

92

93

94

Bring the needle and thread out at A (Figure 92), insert the needle at B, come out at C; go back in at A, out at D, back in at A. Going down the stem, come out at E, back in at A, out at F, and back to E. Come out at G, go back in at E, and come out at H. Go back to E, come out at I, and so on.

Have you seen bird tracks on the sand? They look like individual Fern Stitches! (Figure 93.)

The Fern Stitch is a good stitch to practice working freehand without drawing lines first. It is a good doodling stitch. You can, for instance, make a sprig of Fern Stitches with a heavy yarn. Then take a finer thread of a different color and go back over the same stitches, letting the thread fall wherever it wants to, or thread both yarns in the needle at the same time (Figure 94). How about threading under the Straight Stitches? You can add Long Stemmed Knots. Just start and you will have a lot of fun.

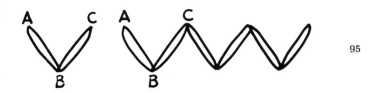

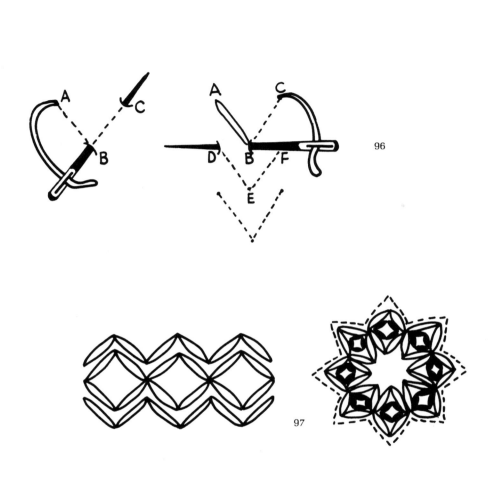

ARROWHEAD STITCH

The Arrowhead Stitch is like a Fern Stitch with two sides instead of three. You can make individual ones, or work lines in any direction you want (Figure 95).

Bring the needle and thread out at A (Figure 96), go in at B, out at C, then go back in at B. If you are working Arrowhead Stitches under each other, continue by coming out at D, in at E, out at F, back in at E, and so on. If you want to work the stitches next to each other, holding hands, you can either complete each stitch before going on to the next or you can work it as a Zigzag Double Running Stitch.

Arrowhead Stitch can be the foundation of interesting designs (Figure 97). It is useful to fill shapes quickly.

Aase, age 10, first drew her owl on paper and then redrew it on burlap, outlining the shape in brown wool Chain Stitch. The wings were a problem. With brown yarn doubled, she tried Satin Stitches at first, but the stitches were too long and too heavy; she felt that too much yarn was wasted on the back. Aase said, "It ended by my making up a stitch," and a most effective stitch it is. She demonstrated it: "I first made a cross; then, picking up a small amount of material, I always crossed over the last stitch; that way most of the thread was on the front." And so it was, a sort of free-form Herringbone which gave a feathered effect. She edged her piece with long and short Blanket Stitch. (Photograph by Don Normark.)

HERRINGBONE STITCH

The Herringbone Stitch goes quickly once you understand how to work it. You can use it in many different ways. As Aase explained it when she worked her owl: "You first make sort of a cross, then you always cross your last stitch." In working her stitches in a free way, Aase obtained an interesting feather texture for her owl.

To learn the mechanics of the Herringbone Stitch, it is a good idea to first practice it on a material with an even weave, such as two-over-two monk's cloth or a good quality burlap stiffened with spray starch. Think of a square made up of four big fabric threads each way. Work from left to right. Bring your needle and thread out at A (Figure 98), at the bottom left corner of the

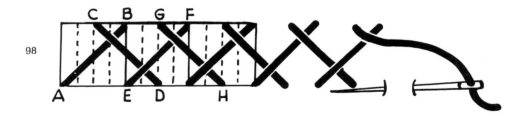

98

99

first square. Go over to B, diagonally across the square. From B go horizontally under to C, half way back to the left. From C, diagonally down to D, half way across the next square. From D, under to E, opposite B; from E over to F, under to G (opposite D), down to H, and so on. Very soon, you will be able to work it freely in any direction.

Try picking up smaller stitches (Figure 99), with A in the same starting position as the Closed Herringbone Stitch, not in the corner. Worked in a circle, it becomes one way of expressing the sun.

CLOSED HERRINGBONE STITCH

This is a beautiful, closer together, Herringbone. Watch the diagram, Figure 100, and notice that A is not in the bottom left corner, nor is it under C, but halfway between. If C were directly opposite A, the result would be a slanting Herringbone. Sometime you may want it slanted but first learn it straight. Notice also that E is not opposite B, as in regular Herringbone, but halfway between C and B. After E, you will find that your needle is always moving horizontally from right to left, under two fabric threads. It goes quickly. The back shows two rows of Back Stitches.

The Closed Herringbone Stitch is a wonderful stitch to fill shapes, either one row for filling shapes such as leaves and petals, or several rows for larger shapes. If the stitches are too long, tie them down with Running Stitches, Straight, or Back Stitches (Figure 101). Carla enjoyed doing this for five of her leaves (see page 134). You can also tie them down with Detached Chains. The Mexicans use tight rows of closed Herringbone to outline shapes.

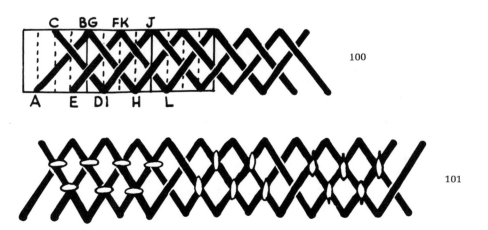

100

101

THE LOOPED STITCH FAMILY

Looped Stitches are quick to work and relaxing. They are easiest to work in the hand without a hoop or frame. They are decorative and can be used to follow lines and fill shapes. Some, like the Blanket Stitch, can be used to go over the outside edges of a stitchery.

Sail boat worked by the author to illustrate the Buttonhole Stitch. The sail to the right was worked Detached.

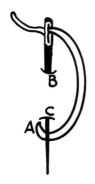
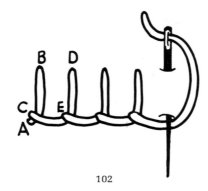

102

BLANKET STITCH AND BUTTONHOLE STITCH

These are the best known Looped Stitches. The only difference between
them is that Buttonhole Stitches are closer together. Work from left to right.
Bring your needle and thread out at A (Figure 102). (If you are working over
an edge, instead of starting with a knot, take two or three very small stitches
from right to left towards A.) Holding the thread down with your left thumb,
the material between your left thumb and first finger, insert the needle at B.
Come out at C, just above and close to A, drawing the needle out over the
thread coming from A to form a loop. (If you are binding an edge, the needle
inserted at B goes from the back of the material over the thread coming from
A.) Going in at D, come out at E, drawing the needle out over the thread
coming from C to make a loop, and so on.

You will enjoy inventing many variations. They can vary in length, in
spacing, and in grouping. Here are a few to try on your doodling cloth (Figure
103). Blanket Stitches can also be worked in a circle with the looped edge on
the inside, which is an easy way to make the sun, or they can be looped on
the outside for flower or wheel designs (Figure 104).

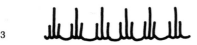

103

104

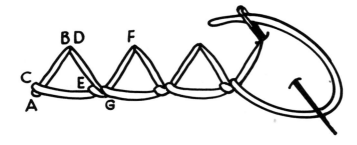

105

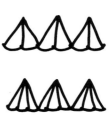

CLOSED BUTTONHOLE STITCH

The Closed Buttonhole is made up of two stitches worked from the same hole, the first one from right to left, the second from left to right, making little triangles (Figure 105). You can have three or four stitches in the same hole.

BUTTONHOLE FILLING

Shapes can be filled in many different ways with rows of Buttonhole Stitches on top of each other (Figure 106).

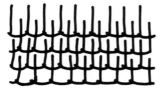

106

107

DOUBLE BUTTONHOLE STITCH

This is made up of two rows of Buttonhole or Blanket Stitches facing each other (Figure 107). First work one row from left to right. At the end of the row, turn your work around and work the second row, fitting in between the arms of the first row. You can use the same color, two different colors, or try it with the same color, but one light and one dark.

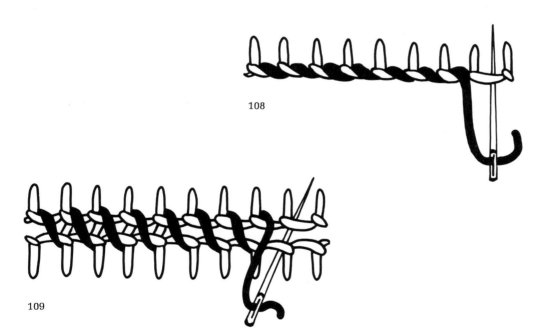

108

109

WHIPPED BUTTONHOLE

When you want to bring in another color, don't forget that stitches can be Whipped (Figure 108). Try two rows of stitches back to back and whip them together (Figure 109).

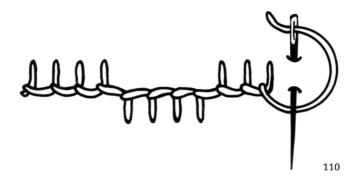

110

OUTLINE BUTTONHOLE STITCH

This is a good stitch for textured outlines, especially furry animals or feathers. It can be worked on either side of the line or on alternate sides. Work from left to right (Figure 110) with the needle picking up material straight up and down, always pointing towards the line on either side. Filling spaces with Seed Stitches or French Knots makes an interesting border (Figure 111). It is a quick way to make little trees (Figure 112).

111

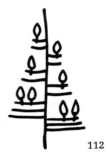

112

SINGLE FEATHER STITCH

The Single Feather Stitch is really an Outline Buttonhole Stitch, slanting instead of straight.

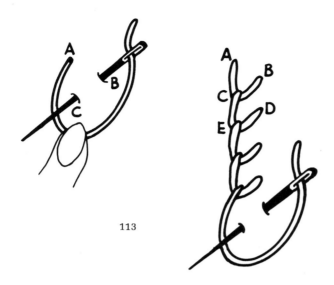

113

Work from the top down, towards you (Figure 113). Bring the needle and thread out at A on the line you want to cover. Holding the thread coming from A down with your left thumb, loop it towards the right and insert the needle at B, on the right side, and come out at C, under A. Draw the needle and thread over the looped thread. Start again, holding the thread down, loop towards the right, insert the needle at D, under B, and come out at E, under C. Loop the thread coming from C under the point of the needle and pull through, and so on.

CRETAN STITCH

The Cretan Stitch is a looped stitch very much like the Outline Buttonhole Stitch worked on one side, then the other, except that instead of coming out on a center line the stitches come out on two parallel lines. You will find the stitch very useful to fill shapes because you can change width as you go along; you can work it close together for a solid effect or space it for a light feeling. It is the stitch Curt used across the middle of his fish as a solid band; following the weave of the burlap made it easy for him (see page 75).

The Cretan Stitch is named after the Island of Crete because the people living there used it for centuries. It is best to learn it first on a coarse-weave material, such as burlap or monk's cloth, and to work it first in a regular pattern. As soon as you understand the rhythm of it you can work it irregularly, close together or with spaces between, any width you want. We all have favorite stitches or favorite ways of using a stitch. My special stitch combination, almost a trade mark with me, is to work the Cretan Stitch between two rows of Chain Stitches, working right through the middle of the chains. It gives a very neat edge (Figure 114). (See next page.)

114

Detail from a Celtic scroll design worked in two
values of red on a white blouse. The stitch is close
Cretan, between two rows of Chain Stitch. (Worked
by the author.)

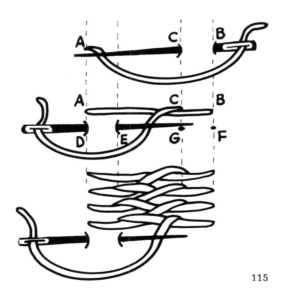

115

Work from left to right or from top down. If you are learning on burlap or
monk's cloth, work over eight threads of the cloth (two on the left, four in
the middle, two on the right). If the material is too fine for this, draw lines as
marked on Figure 115.

Bring the needle and thread out at A on the left side (Figure 115). Loop
your thread down and to the right and insert at B on the opposite side, taking

98

a small horizontal stitch to C. Pull through with the thread from A looped under the needle. Next loop your thread down and to the left, insert at D under A and come out at E with the thread from C looped under the needle. Pull through. With the thread down, insert at F, out at G, and continue from side to side with the needle always pointing from the outside edge in towards the middle and over the looped thread. It looks difficult but you will acquire a rhythm very quickly. Make the effort to learn it and you will love it.

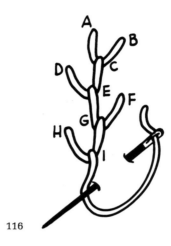

116

SPINE STITCH

When you work the Single Feather Stitch, first on one side, then on the other side, you get the Spine Stitch. Start by working a Single Feather Stitch on the right side (Figure 116), from A to B to C. Then loop your thread to the left, hold it down with your left thumb, and insert the needle at D, opposite C. Come out slanting down at E, straight under C. Draw the needle over the looped thread coming from C. Now loop your thread again to the right, hold it down, insert the needle at F, opposite E, come out slanting down at G over the looped thread. Pull through. Loop your thread to your left, insert at H, come out at I, and so on. You can work it close together, to get a spine, or you can work it open and free. It can look like ferns and other growing things (Figure 117).

117

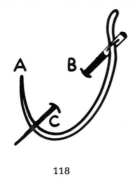

118

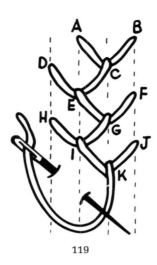

119

120

SLANTING FEATHER STITCH

This is the best known stitch of the Feather Stitch family. It is a good idea to practice it with thick yarns on a coarse material with definite lines. Two-over-two monk's cloth makes learning easier.

Bring the needle and thread out at A (Figure 118). Looping your thread to the right, insert at B opposite A, slanting the needle from B to C, come out at C and loop the thread from A under the point of the needle. Pull through. Now loop your thread to the left, insert at D opposite C (Figure 119), coming out at E, under A; pull through. Loop your thread to the right, insert at F, under B, coming out at G, under C, and so on, looping your thread first on one side, then on the other. Instead of the needle coming out on a center line as for the Spine Stitch, it comes out in a zigzag line, C E G I K.

There are many variations you can discover. You can work Feather Stitches straight up and down, close together or far apart. After you have practised with thick yarns, try thin ones for different effects. A good way to develop spontaneous stitching is to work a branch of Slanting Feather Stitches, then add to it by threading around the ends with a lighter shade, up one side, down the other (Figure 120), with arms apart or joined together. Think of other stitches you can add, such as Stemmed Knots. In no time you can create beautiful designs, one step at a time.

FLY STITCH

The Fly Stitch is a great favorite of mine because it is easy and can be used in many ways. Bring the needle and thread out at A (Figure 121). Hold the thread down with the left thumb, looping it towards the right. Insert at B, coming out at C, below, halfway between A and B. The thread is looped under the point of the needle from left to right; pull it through over the loop. Anchor down by inserting at D. You can anchor it with a small stitch, or a long one, a knot, or with a Detached Chain, in which case it becomes known as the *Tête de Boeuf* Stitch, which means Ox Head Stitch (Figure 122).

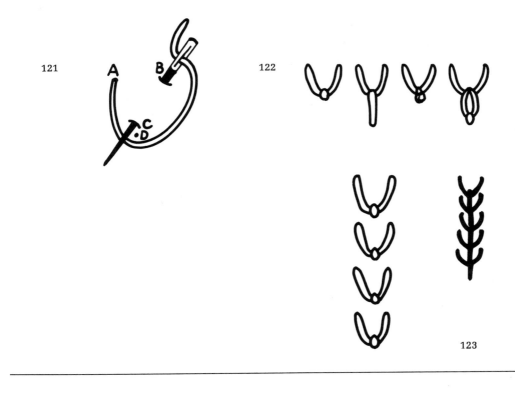

121

122

123

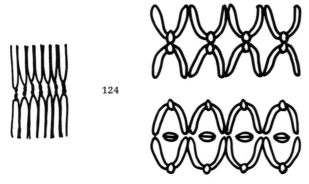

124

125

The Fly Stitch can be worked detached or close together, one above the other (Figure 123). You can have the stitches holding hands, back to back, or facing each other, (Figure 124). Rows can be overlapped to create textures and fill shapes, with variations in color or weight of thread (Figure 125). You

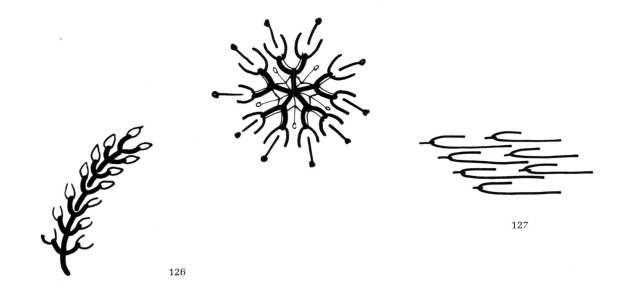

126

127

can whip it or lace it. It can also become the base for threaded stitches and to express growing forms (Figure 126). How about making one side long and the other short (Figure 127)?

CROWN STITCH

A variation of the Fly Stitch is the Crown Stitch, made by anchoring the Fly Stitch with an extra stitch on each side (Figure 128). You can make up interesting designs with the Crown Stitch. Try Long Stemmed Knots as anchoring stitches (Figure 129). Stitches can be threaded through the anchoring stitches or through the arms.

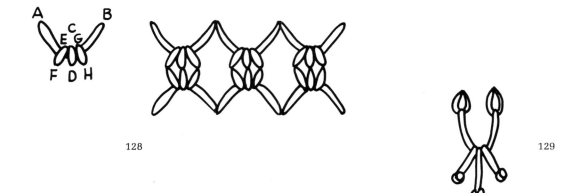

128

129

CHAINED STITCHES

Chained Stitches are good to outline shapes as well as to fill them. The children in Chijnaya in Peru make delightful murals, showing life as it is in their village, working spontaneously on their home-spun wool. For four years the regular Chain Stitch was the only stitch they knew (see page 23). Chained Stitches are easiest to learn by using a firm thread such as a pearl cotton.

CHAIN STITCH

Working towards you, bring the needle and thread out at A at the top of the line you intend to cover (Figure 130). Holding the thread down with the left thumb, loop the thread towards the right. Insert the needle again in the same hole at A and come out at B, with the thread under the point of the needle from left to right and draw the needle through. Again hold the thread down with your left thumb, loop it towards the right, insert the needle at B inside the chain, in the same hole, keeping the thread looped down from left to right. Come out at C, loop the thread under the needle from left to right and draw through. Repeat on and on. Learn to make even, relaxed stitches. If you pull too hard, the cloth will pucker; if you don't pull enough, the stitches will look untidy. Look at the back of your work and you will, I hope, see a row of even Back Stitches. At the end of the row, anchor the last chain down with a little stitch just below the last chain.

   Very young children and some handicapped children find the Chain Stitch difficult. Try giving them a curved needle (See Needles, page 165), working away from the body rather than towards it (Figure 131). Another approach is to teach them the Broad Chain described on page 105.

131

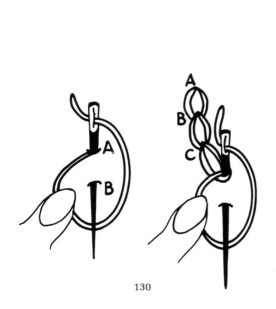

130

Diana, 11, loves horses. She obtained an excellent texture by using various weights of brown string and brown threads, doubling the finer ones. Because she had a strong unconscious feeling for texture, Diana worked the Chain Stitch with a slight twist, by inserting the needle a little higher than the spot from which it came out. This is particularly effective on the back of the head. A wise teacher let her give her own interpretation to the Chain Stitch.

CHAIN STITCH VARIATIONS

When Diana filled the head of her horse with Chain Stitches, instead of inserting the needle in the same hole, she inserted it above where it first came out. This gave a different twist to the stitch (Figure 132). Some people insert the needle a little to the right of A. Again this makes the stitch a little different (Figure 133). Why don't you try various ways of working the stitch?

You can vary the length of your stitches, long and short or one long and two shorts (Figure 134). Using another color, you can work Running Stitches or Back Stitches in the middle of the Chain (Figure 135). You can work an-

132

133

134

135

136

137

138

139

other row of chains over the first, using a finer thread (Figure 136). You can fill the chains with Seed Stitches, French Knots, or work Straight Stitches over the sides, straight or slanting, as in Figure 137. These are good ways to introduce other colors. The chain can be Whipped on one side (Figure 138), on both sides, or the whole chain can be whipped; it can also be threaded. Several close rows can be whipped together (Figure 139).

BROAD CHAIN

For children who find the regular Chain Stitch difficult to learn, there are other ways of obtaining a similar effect, for instance, with the Broad Chain or the Divided Chain. These are easy to learn. They are beautiful and follow curves easily.

The Broad Chain is really a Reverse and Threaded Chain Stitch. Work towards you. Bring the needle and thread out at A (Figure 140) and take a small stitch from A to B. Come out at C, below B, and pull through. Now, pass the needle behind the stitch AB, from right to left, "under the bridge,"

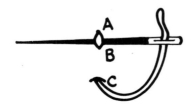

140 continued on next page

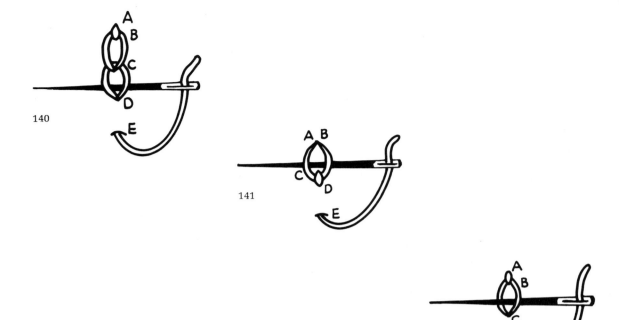

140

141

142

without picking up material. Insert again at C and come out at D. Pull through gently. Pass the needle from right to left under the chain BC, without picking up any material; insert at D, come out at E. Pull through gently. Pass the needle behind the chain CD, and so on. It is easy to follow curves with the Broad Chain. The Broad Chain can also be started with a Detached Chain and go behind the chain ABCD (Figure 141).

LINK CHAIN

For a change, try sliding the needle under half the chain (Figure 142), under the right side only instead of both sides, with the needle going over the left side of the chain. The result is a great favorite of mine, the Link Chain. One side is a little more raised than the other.

DETACHED CHAIN

Instead of a row of chains, each chain can be by itself, anchored with a small stitch at the bottom of the loop (Figure 143). It is then called Detached Chain or Lazy Daisy.

143

144

145

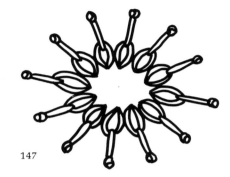

146

147

Another way of anchoring the loop is with a long stitch, a knot, or a Long Stemmed Knot (Figure 144). If the chain is a large size, you can work a smaller Detached Chain inside with a different thread or color. Try using very thick thread for a fat chain or a thin thread for a long narrow chain (Figure 145). It is fun to try out spontaneous designs and invent textures on your doodling cloth (Figures 146-147).

TWISTED CHAIN

For a different, slightly rough texture, try inserting the needle to the left of each last stitch instead of in the same hole, crossing over the thread. This gives a twist to the chain.

Working towards you, bring the needle and thread out at A, on the line you want to cover (Figure 148). Holding the thread down with the left thumb and looping it from left to right, insert at B, to the left of A. Slant your needle downward to C, below A. Loop the thread coming from A over the needle and then under the point of the needle from left to right. Pull through. Hold your thread down as before, insert at D, outside the chain to the left of C, coming out at E, and so on.

If you work rows of Twisted Chain close together, you will make an interesting texture. Note the similarity between Twisted Chain and Coral Knot.

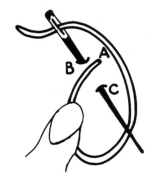

148

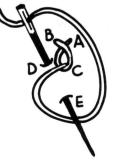

149

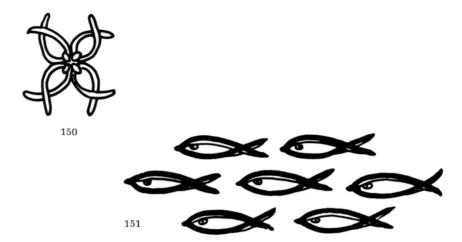

150

151

You can also work each Twisted Chain Detached, anchoring it as in Figure 149. Try it for geometric designs, for seed pods, schools of little fish (Figures 150-151). For the fish you might thread together a heavy green yarn with a thin blue one.

DIVIDED CHAIN STITCH

When children find the regular Chain Stitch difficult, especially inserting the needle in the previous chain, try the Divided Chain, which seems easier for some. There are two ways of working it; each has its own character.

Thread two equal lengths of yarn together (doubling the yarn does not work as well), and tie the ends together in a knot. Now start as you did for the Stem or Outline Stitch (page 83). Work from left to right or if it seems easier, point the needle away from you. Bring your needle and thread out at A (Figure 152); then with the point of the needle and your left thumb, separate the two threads, one up, one down. Between the two threads, go in at B, and come out at C, halfway between AB. Pull through. Again separate your two threads and, between them, go in at D and out at B. Pull through. Sepa-

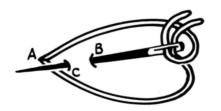

152

153

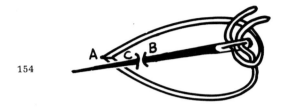

154

rate and go in at E, out at D, and so on. Isn't it a neat, full chain? (Figure 153).

The other way of working the Divided Chain is to pick up a small amount of material instead of going back to the previous hole (Figure 154). This makes a different, interesting texture and is economical of thread since there is so little on the back. That was the way Clarice Ryan's students worked the wave scroll on the edge of their Peruvian mural. It went quickly; there is hardly any yarn on the back, and the effect is good.

THREADED SQUARE CHAIN

The regular Square Chain is a little difficult to work well, but you can get exactly the same effect by threading, which is easy. It becomes a Reversed Square Chain. As one child put it, "It's easier this way — I can tell better which way I'm going."

You can work it in any direction you like. I find it easiest to work from right to left. Start with two Straight Stitches, one under the other, A to B, C to D, like the top and bottom of a square (Figure 155). (If you like, you can add a Straight Stitch from B to C.) From D, go under to E, to the left of DC. Slide the needle upward under the two bridges, DC and AB, without picking up any material. Insert your needle at F, come out at G; pull through gently, not tightly. Slide the needle upward under the two bridges ED and FA, insert at H, come out at I, and so on.

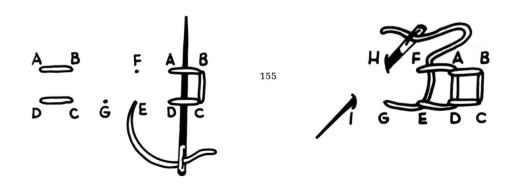

155

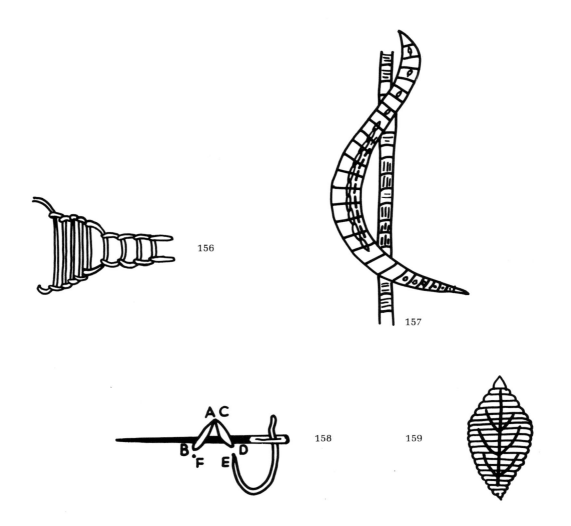

156

157

158   159

After you have practiced a little, try making your stitches longer, shorter, close together, farther apart (Figure 156). This is one of the best stitches I know for learning to be free with a needle. It can follow lines or fill shapes. You can fill the spaces inside the chain with Straight Stitches, horizontal or vertical, with Seed Stitches, Detached Chain, or French Knots. You can go over the Square Chain with Running Stitches or Chain Stitches (Figure 157). It can also be used to couch heavy yarns.

If you want to start a pointed design, like filling a leaf shape, work two stitches from one point (Figure 158), then start threading. Long stitches on a wide leaf can be couched down (Figure 159). You can start a design with a Broad Chain, then widen it into a Threaded Square Chain. Look at pictures of the work of Mariska Karasz and see what she did with the Square Chain.

110

In this Hungarian cushion cover, the Square Chain is used entirely in its conventional form. The Hungarians call it "the big writing stitch" or "the little writing stitch," depending on the width of the stitch. They work it with a soft cotton, usually a true red or a royal blue. This piece would be called "embroidery," rather than "stitchery."

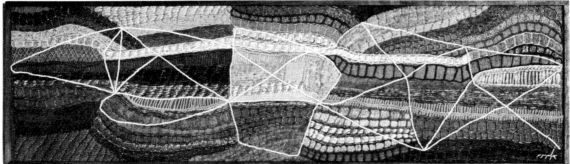

THE CRUISE by Mariska Karasz. Mariska Karasz was born and raised in Hungary, coming to the United States as a young girl. In her native country, the Square Chain is almost a national stitch. It was natural that she should bring it with her. She used it a great deal. What she did that was new and different was to free it from its traditional form and use it as an art form. This free use of stitches as an art form has become known as "Stitchery," rather than embroidery. (From the author's collection.)

Sampler by Mariska Karasz. I like to think of this joyful piece as a doodling cloth on which the artist experimented with stitches, colors, and textures. It is a magnificent lesson in the use of stitches and is one of my most prized possessions! (From the author's collection.)

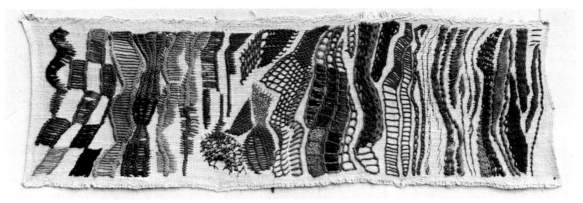

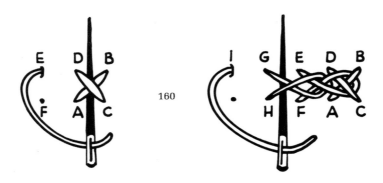

160

VANDYKE STITCH

The Vandyke Stitch is very much like the Threaded Square Chain except that the stitches are crossed instead of straight. It tends to pucker the material, so work it relaxed or keep the material taut in a hoop or frame.

Work from top down or right to left. Start with a cross, bringing the needle and thread out at A (Figure 160), insert diagonally across to B, down under to C, and over diagonally across to D. From D, go under to the left, come out at E and pull through gently. Next slide your needle upward under the cross without picking up any material. Go in at F, below E. Come out at G, to the left of E. Slide the needle upward under the last crossed threads; in at H, out at I, and so on.

You will find many uses for the Vandyke Stitch by varying the length of the stitches. It makes a good edge for a furry animal. Try it with long arms on one side, short arms on the other; also with no arms at all — it then becomes a raised braid or raised outline. Once you understand the rhythm of the Vandyke Stitch, it goes very quickly.

MAGIC CHAIN

This stitch is also called the Checkered Chain. Use two yarns of different color, such as red and white; you can also use different weights or textures. Thread them together in the same needle and knot the ends together. I have a red and white thread in my needle.

Start as an ordinary chain, working towards you. Bring the needle and two threads out at A (Figure 161). Push the red thread from A to the side. Holding the white yarn down with your left thumb, insert the needle at A again, come out at B. Loop the white thread from left to right under the point of the needle and pull through, tugging at the red thread a little. You will have one

161

161 continued

white chain. Push the white thread aside, hold the red thread down, insert the needle at B, come out at C. Loop the red thread under the point of the needle from left to right. Pull through, giving a little tug to the white thread. Continue, always pushing aside the yarn used in the last chain, making a chain with the other color. Don't you think there's magic in it? Try to invent variations of your own (Figure 162).

162

LOOPED DETACHED CHAIN

This stitch gives a looped third dimensional texture. Two yarns are threaded together in the same needle. Starting as you did for the Magic Chain, bring the needle and two threads out at A (Figure 163). Insert at A again, with the needle coming out at B. Loop the white thread from left to right under the point of the needle and hold the red thread down, but OVER the needle, with your left thumb. Pull through. As you pull, adjust the red loop to the size you want by pulling on the red thread as it comes out at B. Anchor the white chain down as a Detached Chain at C.

163

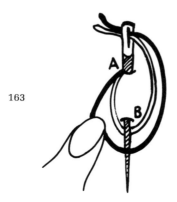

164

165

The anchored chain can be quite large with smaller loose loops (Figure 164), or the anchored chain can be small with larger loose loops. It is fun to make butterflies this way with detached wings (Figure 165). This is the stitch used by the boys for the native's hair, page 142, to give it dimension and texture.

The Looped Detached Chain can also be worked with three threads of different texture and color, anchoring one and adjusting the two loose loops to varying sizes.

KNOTTED STITCHES

Knotted Stitches are useful because their rough, nubby texture makes an interesting contrast to smooth lines. They can follow lines. They can be scattered far apart or close together, or they can fill a shape completely.

If you think of a sunflower, the petals are smooth and even; the center, on the contrary, is rough. Large knots close together would be a good way to give that nubby feeling to the center. If you find knots too difficult, work a short, round Detached Chain with heavy yarn instead. It gives a similar effect.

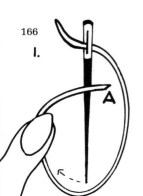

166

I.

FRENCH KNOT

The easiest way to learn to make good French Knots is to have the material stretched taut in a hoop or on a frame and to use a heavy thread.

Bring the needle and thread out at A (Figure 166, Step 1). Swing your thread to the left of A, circle it down from left to right and hold it flat on the material with your left thumb at a place about an inch to the left of A. With your right hand, hold the needle by the eye and slide the point downward "under the bridge" without picking up any material (Step 1). Now think of a

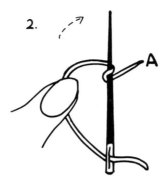

2.

clock: your needle should be pointing to 6 o'clock. Still holding the needle by the eye, turn the point of the needle clockwise, over the thread held by your left thumb, until it points to 12 o'clock (Step 2). Continue to hold the thread down with your left thumb. Insert the point of your needle very close to A but not in the same hole (Step 3). Now gently pull the thread with your left thumb and index finger to snug it around the needle. Push the needle straight down with your right hand (Step 4) and pull through. You should have a neat, firm, well rounded knot. If you pull too hard on loose material the knot may disappear to the back! Practice a few knots so that you understand how they are made and make them easily. If you want bigger knots, use two, three, or more threads at the same time. Try threading the needle with several yarns of different colors or a dark and light yarn of the same color. Use French Knots to anchor Fly Stitches or Detached Chains (Figure 167).

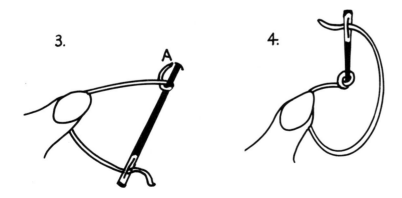

3.

4.

167

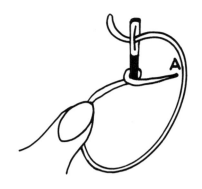

169

168

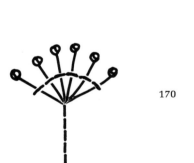

170

171

LONG STEMMED KNOTS

Long Stemmed Knots are useful for small flowers, for stamens on flowers, and for many designs (Figure 168). Start exactly as for a regular French Knot (Figure 166, Steps 1 and 2). When your needle points to 12 o'clock, slide it sideways to where you want the knot to be and insert there, leaving a stem (Figure 169). If the stems are too long, they tend to be untidy. In that case, tack them down with a little stitch: this can become part of your design (Figure 170). Use Long Stemmed Knots to anchor Fly Stitches or Detached Chains (Figure 171). Try them for border designs (Figure 172).

172

CORAL KNOT

The Coral Knot follows lines and gives them a decorative, nubby texture. The knots can be quite close together or spaced. If the knots are used to fill a shape, you can make patterns by placing the knots of one line under the spaces of the line above.

Work from right to left. Bring the needle and thread out at A (Figure 173). With your left thumb, hold the thread down on the line to be covered. Insert the needle just above the thread at B, take a slanting small stitch, and come out just below the line at C. The thread from A goes over the needle, then is looped under the point, from left to right. Snug up the thread around the needle and pull through. Repeat for the next knot, and so on. The spacing of the knots depends on the effect you want; the size varies with the thickness of the yarn. You can make BC, DE straight up and down instead of slanting; try each way and see which one fills your need. In old English books the slanting Coral Stitch is called Snail-Trail!

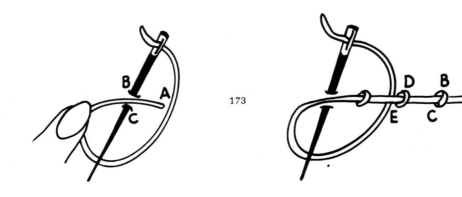

173

COUCHING

After Straight Stitches, Couching is perhaps the first spontaneous stitch to be "invented" by children. A stitch is too long, so they "tack it down" or "stake it down": that is Couching. It is a most satisfying way of expressing a feeling or an idea because it requires no special knowledge or skill. Who doesn't love to make pictures on damp sand with the end of a stick, carefree doodlings? Well, Couching is rather like that. You can lay any yarn on material and coax it into any line or shape you want, without any drawing, and then tack it down, either with a similar thread or a completely different one.

Couching is one of the oldest stitches in the world; it is very useful if you want to use heavy yarns, which are too thick to go through the material easily, or for fragile threads such as metal threads. And how else could Kathy (see Color Page 30, C-7) keep her smoke and fluffy clouds in place! Any type of yarn, or several yarns of different textures and colors bunched together, can be used to follow any line you have in mind, or even to fill shapes. You will find it easiest if the material you work on is taut — either well starched or, best of all, stretched on a frame the size of your picture. This is how 9-year-old Eileen designed her cat (see Color Page 39, C-15); the green burlap was stretched over a homemade frame and stapled to the back. This shows well the advantage of being able to see the picture as a whole before stitching. It is one of the best approaches to creating spontaneously with stitches.

If the yarn to be couched is not too heavy, the beginning and the end can be pulled through to the back. You can pin it in a few places so as not to lose the line you have in mind. Bring the needle and tacking thread out at A (Figure 174). Go over the yarn you are couching and go in at B, out at C, in at D, out at E, in at F, and so on.

174

Many stitches can be used to do the couching: groups of Straight Stitches, Cross Stitches, Buttonhole, Threaded Square Chain, Fly Stitches, Long Stemmed French Knots (Figure 175). The couched yarn can go in any direction: it can be coiled (Figure 176), it can zigzag (Figure 177). If the yarn is loose and bulky, you can couch it down from place to place, using a fine thread, pulling it around with tight, close stitches to form a thin line, then leaving it free and a little loose in other places before tacking it down again (Figure 178). It makes me think of spring, of round buds ready to burst, and of pussywillows. Mariska Karasz used Couched Stitches a great deal. In some pieces, such as "Telephone Lines," she used Couched Stitches almost exclusively.

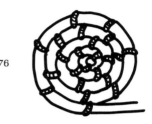

177

178

TELEPHONE LINES by Mariska Karasz.
(Courtesy of Mrs. Solveig Cox, Alexandria, Virginia.)

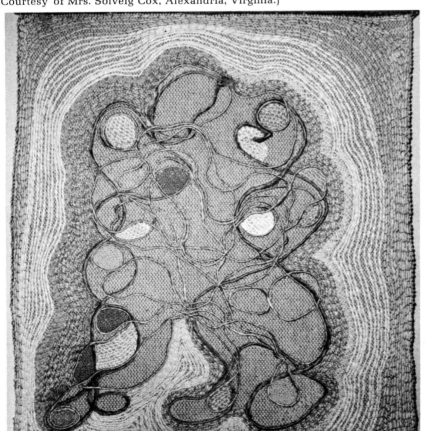

Jane Wirtz made excellent use of the Bokhara Stitch for her delightful snail. The shell is worked in five values of burnt coral yarn; the head is gold. The snail is beaming at a little slug "who turned green with envy."

ROUMANIAN, NEW ENGLAND LAID, AND BOKHARA COUCHING

Another way of couching stitches is to tack each stitch down as you work it, using the same yarn. This can be done in a number of ways. When the thread to be couched is not too long, you can tack it down with one stitch across the middle; this is the Roumanian Stitch.

Work from top down, bringing the needle and thread out at A on the left (Figure 179). Go in at B and come out at C, just a little above AB, not quite half way across. Pull through. Take a small diagonal stitch over AB to D. This "tacks down" AB and holds it in place. Start the next stitch coming out at E, going over to F and out at G, in line with C, and in at H. Come out at I, over to J, and so on. For a change you can make the tacking stitches straight up and down.

The pioneer women of New England made up their own variation of the Roumanian Stitch, with the tacking-down stitch CD quite long. It is called the New England Laid Stitch (Figure 180). Because threads were scarce, these resourceful women found a way of filling shapes, keeping most of the thread on the surface, with very little of it wasted on the back. It produces an interesting texture. Try it sometimes instead of Surface Satin Stitch.

When you couch down a long stitch with several small stitches over it, it becomes the Bokhara Stitch. Follow the diagram (Figure 181). Work a long stitch from A to B, then tack it down with small stitches CD-EF-GH-IJ; follow with another long stitch, KL, tacked down MN, OP, and so on. Rows of Bokhara Stitches side by side make a good solid filling. It is a quick way to fill a large shape.

Roumanian, New England Laid, or Bokhara Stitches can be worked with the threads close together or they can be spaced. The tacking stitches can be part of the design.

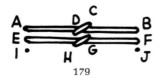

179

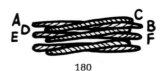

180

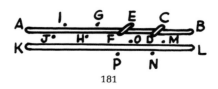

181

SPLIT LAID WORK AND PUEBLO EMBROIDERY TECHNIQUE

Many children I know have "invented" their own version of this stitch to fill their need. It is very thrilling to know that the Pueblo Indians of New Mexico and Arizona have used this stitch for centuries to produce a distinctive type of embroidery, completely their own. They call it Pueblo Embroidery Technique. To work it they use a 2-ply twisted yarn, splitting the yarn exactly in two, with the needle. The rows are worked close to each other as a solid filling. This stitch is taught at the Institute of American Indian Arts in Santa Fe, New Mexico. It is used beautifully by American Indian artist Josephine Wapp, to fill large spaces of Pueblo Indian designs.

The stitch, used as a quick line, was "invented" by Carol for the tentacles of her jellyfish. Think of it as the Long Stem Stitch, splitting the yarn as you come out.

Sacred kilt, Zuni, New Mexico, worked in Pueblo Embroidery Technique. The back shows how only a small amount of yarn is wasted on the back. (Courtesy of the Smithsonian Institution.)

When 11-year-old Carol "invented" Split Laid Work for the tentacles of her jellyfish, she had no idea that long before her time Southwest American Indians used the stitch to fill their need. Carol's "underwater" stitchery was worked freehand; the jellyfish is almost moving as you watch it.

Scarf of hand-woven cotton embroidered in Pueblo Embroidery Technique by Josephine Wapp, using blue and red yarn. Miss Wapp prefers to use natural dyes "because they are easier to blend; also they are beautiful." Her craftsmanship is superb. (Courtesy of Josephine Wapp, Santa Fe, New Mexico.)

Work from left to right, towards you, or away from you, whichever seems easiest. Use a sharp needle. Working from left to right, bring the needle and thread out at A (Figure 182). Insert at B and take a very small stitch backwards to C. As the point of your needle comes out at C, hold the thread from A flat on the cloth with your left thumb over the line to be covered and let the point split the yarn exactly in two. Pull through. Continue, inserting the needle at D and letting the point come out backwards at E, splitting the yarn in two. It goes quickly and there is very little thread wasted on the back, which makes it economical to use. Although the diagram shows the needle coming in and out, if the stitchery is stretched on a frame, work the stitch by stabbing straight down and straight up. The yarn is split in two as you come back up. You can work several rows close together to fill à shape as the Pueblo Indians do and as Josephine Wapp did on her scarf. She says she works it "usually from bottom up, and back down." It is interesting to try it zigzag (Figure 183). If you make the zigzag stitches very short you will get an attractive textured line which has many creative possibilities. I "discovered it" while I was doodling with needle and thread, trying to express an odd weed I had seen.

183

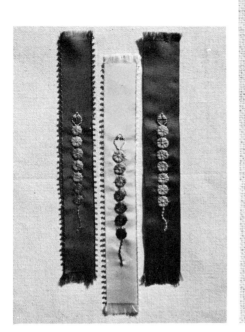
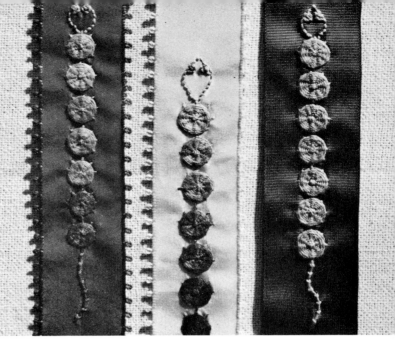

Bookworm bookmarks by the author, worked in Woven Spider Web Stitch.

SPIDER WEB STITCH

Few stitches are more striking than the Spider Web Stitch. There are many ways of working it. Here are two easy ways:

WOVEN SPIDER WEB STITCH

First work an odd number of Straight Stitches from one center, pointing out, like the spokes of a wheel. The larger the wheel the more spokes you need. Start with 7 stitches (Figure 184). Later you can try 5 or 9.

Bring the needle and thread out at A in the center and insert at B, then under and back out again at A. If you start with a knot, be careful to hold it under the material to one side so as not to poke into it as you come up from the center. I like to start without a knot, leaving a short length of thread on the back side and tying it after the web is woven. Insert at C, back out at A, then insert at D, and so on around to H.

184

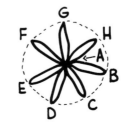

123

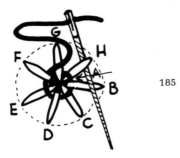

185

To weave, bring the needle and the same thread (or a different thread) out at A (Figure 185) and weave over and under the spokes. Pull the thread snugly at first around the center, then relax a little as you work outward. If you want to use an even number of spokes and the weaving stitches get to be a little long, they can be couched down part of the way with Straight Stitches and Long Stemmed Knots (Figure 186), or with Long Stemmed Detached Chain. These can in turn be threaded for added dimension. Try to create new patterns.

186

RIBBED SPIDER WEB STITCH

First lay the spokes of your web as you did for the Woven Spider Web except that you can have an even number of spokes if you want to. Start with 6 spokes (Figure 187). To fill the web, bring the needle and thread out at A between B and C. Take a step backwards and slide the needle under AB and AC. Pull through snugly. Continue taking a step backwards under AC and

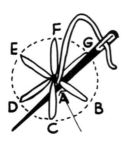

187   continued on next page

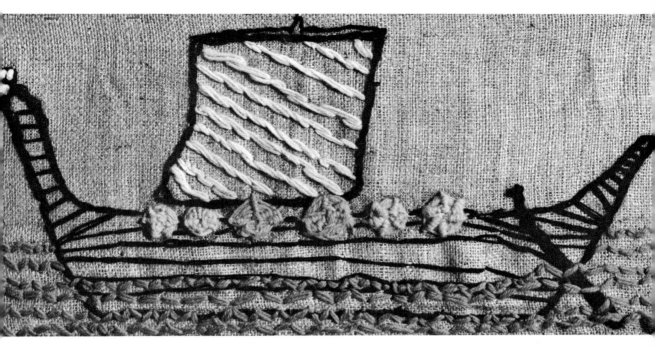

THE DEAD VIKING SHIP. Said 10-year-old Scott: "I did a Viking ship because my ancestors were Norwegian. I love ships and I wanted a long, narrow piece of burlap. so I thought of this ship. It's a dead Viking ship; in a battle everybody was killed. They just left the ship there and it just drifted away. I just drew it freehand on the cloth. It was fun to think up stitches. I used the Spider Web for the shields. It wasn't too even at first but I ended up by being pretty good at it." (Photograph by Don Normark.)

AD, backwards under AD and AE, and so on around as many times as necessary. You will see little ridges forming on the spokes of your web. You can fill it up or leave some of the spokes showing.

DETACHED STITCHES

You can invent all sorts of exciting uses for Detached Stitches. They are worth learning, especially if you use heavy threads. Some take a little practice to do well. They are worked over Foundation Stitches in such a way that they do not enter the material except at the beginning and at the end. Foundation Stitches can be Straight Stitches, Outline, Back, Buttonhole — almost any stitch — each one with a different effect.

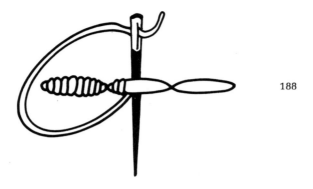

188

DETACHED OVERCAST STITCH

The stitch Eleanor "invented" for her sheep, page 133, was really a Detached Overcast Stitch worked over Back Stitches (Figure 188).

To obtain a continuous raised line, a good foundation is made by working two rows of Long Stem Stitches loosely, the first row, A, BC, DE, FG, with the second row, a, bc, de, fg, worked in the intervals of the first (Figure 189).

189

After the foundation is laid, bring the needle and thread out at A (Figure 190), and whip over and under the two rows of Stem Stitches without picking up material, and with the stitches close to each other.

190

191

192

BUTTONHOLE STITCH BARS

Instead of whipping over and under as for the Detached Overcast Stitch, you can work Buttonhole Stitches over the Foundation Stitches. Work two or three relaxed Straight Stitches, AB, CD, EF (Figure 191), close to each other for a wide bar. For a narrow bar, work CD from the same holes as AB.

Over these stitches, work Buttonhole Stitches close to each other without going through the material, except at the beginning and at the end (Figure 192). This is the way button loops are made. In stitchery they can be used decoratively in groups. The backs of some animals, such as porcupines, could be worked this way.

In Figure 193, two Buttonhole Stitch Bars were made, starting and ending them in the same place. Each is made over two relaxed Straight Stitches, with the looping on the outside. This tends to make the Bars curve a little.

193

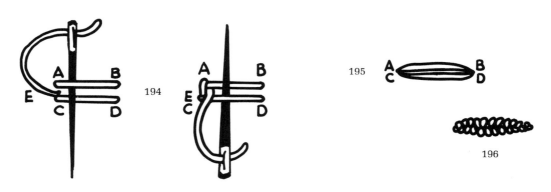

194

195

196

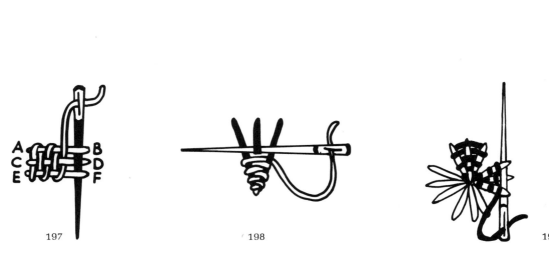

197

198

199

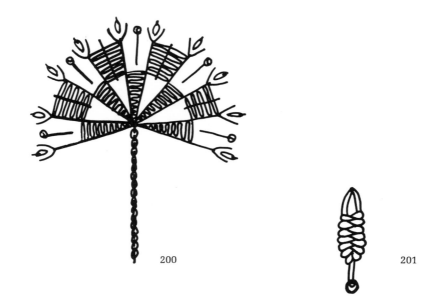

200

201

Needleweaving by William Cahill Johnson. The petals of the flowers were worked over the two sides of a long Detached Chain, weaving from the outside point to the center of the flower. (Photograph by Fred Figgins.)

SUNFLOWER by Esther Feldman. The center of the flower is Ribbed Spider Web Stitch. The petals, in many shades of yellow and gold, are worked in Needle Weaving over long Detached Chains.

WOVEN BARS OR DETACHED NEEDLEWEAVING

These are made over two or three foundation bars of relaxed Straight Stitches worked next to each other (Figure 194).

After two Foundation Stitches are laid, AB and CD, come out at E just above C and start weaving over and under. With the needle pointing down, slide it under AB, over CD. Pull through gently. With the yarn over CD, slide the needle pointing up under CD, over AB. Pull through gently. Continue under AB, over CD, and so on, packing the stitches neatly and evenly side by side.

The two foundation bars can start and end in the same place, with A and C in the same hole, and B and D in the same hole (Figure 195). In this case, the weaving should start and end a little snugly. In France the stitch is called Wheat Stitch because it looks like a grain of wheat (Figure 196).

Try Detached Needleweaving over three parallel Straight Stitches, as in Figure 197, or in a V-shape, with a short Straight Stitch in the middle, as in Figure 198. The stitches should be drawn snugly at the pointed end and gradually relaxed. Weaving over two or three Straight Stitches (Figures 199, 200) can lead to all sorts of exciting designs. An ingenious way of laying Foundation Stitches is used by artist-teacher Esther Feldman. She suggests making long Detached Chains with the weaving worked between the two sides of the chain. Remember that although the Detached Chain is ordinarily anchored with a short stitch it can also be anchored with a French Knot or a

DOUBLE WEAVING by Mariska
Karasz. A beautiful example of
stitches detached from the background cloth. (Courtesy of Mrs.
Solveig Cox. Photograph by Colonel Martin D. McAllister.)

Long Stemmed Knot (Figure 201). Mariska Karasz used Detached Stitches
very effectively in "Double Weaving." Detached Darning (page 60) was used
for "The Holy Family." Use your imagination to discover your own way of
working stitches detached from the cloth, creating new textures. It is very
satisfying to invent your own way of using stitches.

III. Designing Stitcheries

Most children have an inborn sense of design which finds admirable expression in stitchery. It is an excellent medium for their intuitive use of the elements and principles of design. The most satisfactory response will be obtained when they are given a suitable cloth, stretched on a light frame, and a choice of yarns in a variety of textures and colors. The texture of the cloth, the quality of the yarn, their colors, will speak to the child and establish a rapport which will enable him to absorb and create. With little help very young children will unconsciously fill the space with designs that are often beautiful. Results are obtained through direct contact with materials, by "doing" rather than by the academic approach of demonstration, which does not relate to the expression of their feelings. As they stitch, they become absorbed by what is happening under their fingers; they are alert to changes dictated by the stitches and the new textures created. Children seem to be endowed with invisible antennae which suggest the direction of their stitches. Their work is usually simple and honest, fresh and free. (See Color Page 27, C-1.)

The experience of designing stitcheries without a definite subject matter is particularly fruitful when children reach adolescence. The 9- and 10-year-olds slowly become conscious of design; the possibilities intrigue them. It fascinates 11- and 12-year-olds, a good age to crystalize the awareness. They work better in a classroom situation because, out of necessity, the teacher has set up boundaries in advance, such as the type of material, the size of the piece. These limitations act as a stimulus. When there is a definite starting point, when the rules of the game are set, the imagination starts buzzing.

The first step is one of climate, created by an inspiring mother or teacher: enthusiasm and excitement. Next the child should understand that what is important is the feeling he has deep inside himself: the more intense his feeling, the better will his work reflect it. It is good to spend a little time getting acquainted with the cloth, moving collected yarns around within the boundaries, filling the whole area, getting a feel for what the texture and the colors will suggest. Children who have started their first stitcheries in this manner may not need a preliminary sketch and often work directly on the cloth.

The two Peruvian boys had their stitchery boundaries determined in part by the 19-inch width of their handwoven wool background. They usually start with a Chain Stitch frame, in a dark color. By the time this is done, they have had time to decide what the scene is going to be, without any preliminary sketch; they have no paper. They outline in Chain Stitch what they have in mind and fill the shape with colorful yarns, selecting as they go along. (Courtesy of the Andean Foundation.)

Other children need help. If they do, suggest that, whatever they have in mind, the center of interest in their stitchery should be large and simple, stretched to fill the space, one large figure or design rather than several spotty little ones. If the subject is to be tall and thin, use a narrow, vertical piece of cloth. If it is wide and fat or spread out horizontally, use a wide rectangle.

A helpful step is to use heavy yarn or string to develop an awareness of the many things a line can do. The yarn is a line in motion. It can be lazy or active, it can run up or down, wave or zigzag, it can close in on itself and make shapes, beautiful shapes. If the yarn has a mind of its own and seems to be rebellious, why not first see what it wants to say, as it unwinds from the spool, perhaps in waves and loops. These form areas that can be filled with stitches, and shadows which can be stressed. Look at "Telephone Lines"

Theresa, age 11, created her stitchery at home with the idea of working out an abstract design which would make some use of a newly learned stitch, the Threaded Square Chain. Her piece expresses to a remarkable degree the fluid forms of the sea life she was studying at school.

by Mariska Karasz, page 119. If you want an obedient yarn with a more fluid quality, wet it and squeeze the water out between thumb and index finger. This should tame it and take the spring out of it. Hold on to one end and let the other drop on the cloth, creating linear designs. As you do this, think of flowing water, waves, of dancing or flying. Pretend that you are going for a walk and let the yarn respond. Try to determine the general direction of the design, encouraging the yarn into pleasing patterns. It can then be pinned down and couched or used as an indication for a chalk line quickly reinforced with a running or darning stitch. Next to it, or over it, a heavier stitch can start the backbone of the design. When basic lines are established, use your imagination to proceed freehand with stitches.

As the work progresses, it is useful to hold up the stitchery and take a critical look. Perhaps it has too many empty spaces which could be textured with stitches, or it might need a color accent. By praising a child for what he has naturally done well — for instance, the balance of a picture — you develop in him a more conscious awareness of the quality he achieved. He will strive for that quality again and his confidence in himself will grow. Best of all he will sense that you have faith in his ability to express his own ideas in a creative way, that you believe he can produce a good stitchery; and he will.

PLANNING THE DESIGN ON PAPER

Some children prefer to first plan their design on paper. They can do this on several papers the size of the cloth, working as spontaneously as possible and then choosing the best design. Rather than a pencil or crayon, have them use a brush well filled with paint for fluid strokes, not attempting to paint " a line" but letting the feeling flow freely from the arm, the hand, and the brush onto the paper, comfortably filling and dividing the space. The painted brush strokes can be reproduced freehand on the cloth with chalk, or they can be cut out and pinned on the cloth as a pattern for direction; or the painted strokes can be covered with nylon crinoline, traced and reproduced, as explained on page 163.

An exercise students enjoy and find helpful is to close their eyes while they are holding a soft pencil, felt pen, or paint brush in their hand, then

From a visit to the Black Sheep Farm in Suquamish, Washington, Eleanor, age 7, brought back some natural hand-spun embroidery wool to make a stitchery of her favorite sheep, "Pitty Pat." First she made a drawing on paper, then she redrew just the outline freehand with crayon directly on the cloth. Eleanor "invented" a stitch to give a "curly feeling" to the sheep. As she made each back stitch to outline the shape, she went over and under each stitch three or four times, wrapping the wool a little loosely before going on to the next back stitch and repeating the process. She had discovered her own version of the Detached Overcast Stitch. There was one stitch accidentally looser than the others on an ear. The child quickly rationalized: "Oh! that's where Mr. Simmons forgot to clip the wool!"

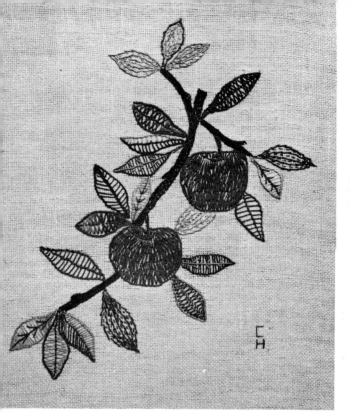

Carla, age 11, is talented. The pink Teddy Bear was her first stitchery. In fifth grade art class at school, she made an attractive water color of an apple branch brought by the teacher. At home during the summer, she used her own painting for the basis of a stitchery. Finding out that the fluid watercolor was not definite enough for a stitchery, Carla used red, green, and brown paper from which she cut out her design, using the pieces as a pattern on burlap stretched on a frame. Wave Stitch was used for the red apples. The leaves gave her the opportunity to practice a number of stitches.

think of a subject (a flower, an animal, a profile . . .) and with their eyes still closed draw the mental picture they have formed. The results are often fresh, free, and can form a good start for a stitchery design.

Another useful approach is with cut paper shapes used as patterns. As early as possible the child should develop the muscular control needed to use scissors freely; it is invaluable in designing for stitchery.

The shapes can be defined, such as squares for houses, rectangles for tall or long houses or trains, triangles for roofs or tepees, circles for balloons, faces, or wheels. Cut in a variety of sizes, they can be used to express many ideas. The mountain goat, page 85, was first cut out in paper shapes. People can be a long thin rectangle with an egg shape on top. Other shapes could be fishes, flowers, leaves, paper-doll people. You might cut through three layers of lightweight paper to play with repetition. The same shape might be repeated in different sizes, perhaps overlapping each other for more interest. The eye enjoys the comforting feeling created by some repetition. See how artist Virginia Tiffany overlapped the bird shapes shown on page 55. Scissors simplify and stylize, omitting unessential details which are apt to lead to photographic representation. Origami folded papers offer another type of simplification, with folded lines to break up the space.

Instead of defined shapes, free-form shapes may fall off the scissors; both the cut-out shape and the resulting negative shapes and scraps can be used. Let the child arrange and rearrange the cut pieces on the cloth to his satisfaction — the eraser-end of a pencil is useful for this — pinning them down and tracing around them. The design can be further emphasized with yarn, couched or used as a line pattern, laid over and between the shapes, relating them so that they form a whole.

Such exercises are particularly fruitful with 12- and 13-year olds, and also with adults who are apt to be inhibited because they think that they cannot draw. These are some of the steps which can be used to experience the elements and the principles of design. But no matter how the stitchery was planned, let it be completely the child's design, interpreted in his chosen stitches. Only in this way can his own stitchery be "very special" for him. The effort he will have made to create will help him to grow and give him self-confidence. It will develop in him an awareness of design and of beauty around him.

USE OF STITCHES IN DESIGN

The designs, the various areas created, provide stimulation for an original use of stitches. It is something that has to be felt. The child who doodles with a needle not only learns the mechanics of new stitches quickly, he also acquires an awareness of what stitches can express. Stitches that are not too planned in advance have vitality; they are responsive to feeling.

Some stitches are best for lines, fluid or solid; other stitches are useful for fillings, scattered or close. Stitches can fill a shape by the use of horizontal, vertical, or diagonal rows, or they can follow the lines of the shape. See how animal shapes were filled by the children of Chijnaya in Peru. Repetition of

Stitchery on homespun wool by the children of Chijnaya, Peru. (Courtesy of Lucille Studebaker, Bellevue, Washington.)

Stitchery by the children of Chijnaya. (From the author's collection.)

Kathy and Karen in stitchery class. (The Needle-craft Shop, Sherman Oaks, California.)

HELEN AND JOHN. Learning new stitches and exploring what she could do with them, Helen Bitar, the artist, made for me this whimsical sampler of stitches which she hoped would appeal to children.

stitches creates textures and patterns. Let the children experience what stitches can do by varying the size; encourage them to practice with different weights and types of thread to create textures. Threading three or four weights and colors together can be quite exciting. Try this for filling a shape with French Knots.

In dealing with texture, avoid placing several busy textures next to each other. It is rather like several people talking out loud at the same time; no one idea stands out and you are left with a feeling of confusion. As contrasting textures are felt, personal variations occur. It is exciting to discover one's own mixture of stitches or one's interpretation of a stitch. For instance, the fuzzy legs on Kathy's caterpillar, worked upside down, show one of the most inspired uses of the Wheat Ear Stitch I have ever seen. There is obviously a close rapport between Kathy and caterpillars. (See Color Page 43, C-21.) (For Wheat Ear Stitch, see *The Stitches of Creative Embroidery.*)

USE OF COLOR

Children have an affinity for color. Their free choice is usually a delight; it is the expression of an emotion, not of a theory; it comes from deep down inside. Give them as many good clear-color yarns as possible. I am always fascinated by the sureness of their choice. As they get older, the intellect gradually takes over from intuition and something is lost. When young children are in the process of selecting colors, there should be no unsolicited suggestion to influence them: they are expressing their own likes and dislikes. An adult choice might be more sophisticated; it is usually not as effective.

During the period when children are losing their fresh, spontaneous approach to color, they can be helped to overcome a creeping feeling of insecurity in designing by playing color games—not by learning theories about color but by experiencing how colors feel and what they do to each other; what colors are warm, what colors are cool. Put a warm yarn next to a cool one, a dark color next to a light color. Place a succession of strong dark-color yarns on a cloth, with clear light colors between, changing them around until you have a pleasing succession — something children often do well.

The nature of the background will influence colors. Take, for instance, a bright, deep-orange yarn. Lay it successively on white paper, on maroon, blue, green, grey, and see how different the orange can look. Next to the orange yarn, place in turn every color yarn you have at hand and see what another color does to orange. Some colors make it sparkle and sing, others make it jump; some make it more intense, others quiet it down. Children bring together unlikely neighbors. A third color may bring harmony or perhaps discord. Shades vary so much in dealing with yarns that there is no substitute for laying them next to each other to make choices.

A doodling cloth is a good place to experiment with stitches in different colors. Try a few Buttonhole Stitches in dark royal blue and put bright red French Knots between; then reverse with red Buttonhole Stitches and royal blue Knots and note the difference. Work a row of deep orange Alternate Stem Stitch and against it a row of yellow. See what red will do to a light yellow-green. Experience a color with three close values next to each other: for instance, a row of dark blue Outline Stitch with a row of medium blue, followed by a light blue, close to it. A row of Double Zigzag Running Stitches in red with a slightly lighter red on the return journey creates a shimmer. See what gold will do to two values of forest green, what blue and green do to each other.

Let the children keep the short lengths of yarns left over from stitching, as many colors as are available, placed in a small transparent plastic bag. When the child feels that perhaps something is lacking in his stitchery, let him lay some of these yarns on his work and move the colors around to see what different colors or textures will do to his piece; perhaps a contrast would improve it. Sometimes little snips of a color — a repeat or an accent — are all that is needed to give the final touch. (See Color Page 39, C-16.) Let them find out the magic of changing something ordinary into something exciting and alive. Color, as experienced in stitchery, can open their eyes to a whole new world.

CHILDREN'S STITCHERY MURALS

Stitchery murals are rewarding and exciting. They provide countless possibilities for group work, whether it be a classroom, a neighborhood group, an organization, or a family project. Ten- to 12-year-olds are particularly responsive to this approach, although children of any age can take part.

A lively discussion of the subject with everyone participating and contributing ideas will create an inspiring atmosphere. The intensity of the stimulation will determine the quality of the result. To spark children into real creativity with needle and thread, the experience must be really lived; the stimulation must be sustained for the duration of the work.

In "Flying Kites," for instance, the boys were really excited about their kites, how gay they would be, how well they would fly. (See Color Page 42, C-19). It was March, kite-flying time in Seattle. The teacher was just as excited as the boys. The stimulation was intense; it carried through into the stitchery.

In the same class, the girls were working on a more static piece, "Mountain Flowers," with scenery of their National Park. Because they were girls, they concentrated on perfect detail, on how to express trees, enjoying the work on flowers. The technique is excellent but the piece does not have the excitement conveyed by the boys in their mural.

Stitchery murals present a challenge to the art teacher. They can play an active part in social studies, providing the children with opportunity for research in depth. The possibilities are endless. A mural could be centered around voyages of discovery, on the Pilgrims and other early settlers in America, on life in other countries, in ancient lands such as Egypt or pre-Columbian Peru. A large map of a country, perhaps England or France, or a map of an American state could be stitched by a group, all working on the outline, followed by individual children stitching representative products or landmarks.

Other themes could originate from vacation projects (see Color Page 43, C-20) or be the result of a class outing. A family mural could spring from the locale of their vacation, from the trip itself by car, train, or plane, with separate parts worked by different members of the family, each with a meaning: a fish caught, flowers and leaves picked, the wasp that stung, the skunk

FLYING KITES. "Flying Kites" was the work of all the boys in Clarice Ryan's class of fifth graders at Viewlands School in Seattle. The idea for the mural came in March, at kite-flying time. The boys pored over four library books on kites, reading and sketching what appealed to them. Each one drew his own kite on a piece of paper and cut it out. These were placed on a large piece of sky-blue burlap, 38 by 44 inches, then shifted around until everyone was pleased with the positions. The outlines were drawn on the cloth, and cotton rug yarns in bright colors were chosen; the work proceeded with two or three boys working at one time, sometimes stitching while they listened as the class recited, other times working during the noon recess. The kite strings were added at the end, freehand, by the three boys whose kites couldn't be used for lack of space. It was altogether a happy and exciting experience for the boys. The finished mural is shown in color on page 42.

Peruvian mural. The sixth grade at Viewlands School in Seattle had been studying early Peruvian civilization. They were fascinated by the pre-Columbian designs they saw in reproductions from the Textile Museum in Washington, D.C., and the Art Institute of Chicago. The girls decided to interpret some of the designs in their own way. They chose a cat, a parrot, a lizard, a ram, and a crayfish, working two of each in opposite directions. With yarns of Peruvian pottery colors — burnt red, ochre, black, gray, and cream — on red burlap rectangles, the girls experimented with stitches to obtain the effect they wanted. The completed rectangles were sewn onto a large, strong neutral background in vertical and horizontal positions.

The teacher, Clarice Ryan, wrote: "This left an empty look so the girls decided first to add a Peruvian wave scroll design on each side. They followed this by working straight black lines around the red pieces. This large piece, 44 by 56 inches, was done in two weeks, mostly in free time and with casual supervision. Never before did I witness able children take work into their own hands in such a possessive way. They knew basic stitches learned in the fifth grade but now they were combining them, experimenting, poring

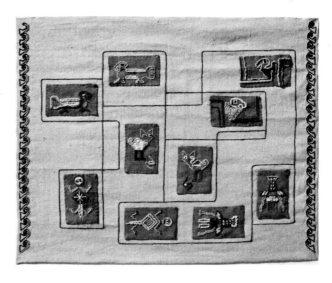

over new stitch diagrams, following directions without any help. They had become really creative."

ALICE IN WONDERLAND. The pupils of the Potomac School, McLean, Virginia, were celebrating the centennial of Lewis Carroll. As their contribu-

tion to the school commemoration, the fifth-grade pupils decided to make an "Alice in Wonderland" stitchery and in so doing carry on the tradition of class murals in the school. (See the NORMAN CONQUEST OF ENGLAND in *The Stitches of Creative Embroidery*.)

Eleanor Poe Barlow, their teacher, writes: "The children, ten girls and ten boys, drew 8- by 8-inch pictures as I read the story to them. They chose a variety of characters and scenes, whatever struck their fancy. We then spent every free moment gathered in small circles, each child with a piece of cloth and a few strands of Persian wool. I taught them approximately 10 to 15 stitches, filling out their samplers, often experimenting on their own. They traced their drawings on layout paper. Each child was given a piece of linen 12 by 12 inches and a piece of dressmaker carbon. The linen was taped to the desk and the design transferred to it. In the weeks that followed, the classroom hummed with happy activity. They took their own pieces home at night. The twenty panels were sewn together around a large, winsome Alice; all the children worked on her as she was on a frame in the classroom. The children are very proud of their stitchery which is now hanging in the school front hall." (Photograph by John Hebeler.)

whose memory lingered on, or remembrances of a visit to a farm, a circus, a Fourth of July picnic. A Sunday School could have a religious theme, The Christmas Story, Noah's Ark. A mural could also be a purely abstract art project.

Murals can be made up of individual pieces joined together. This can still provide a feeling of working as a group, as did "Alice in Wonderland." All

the pieces need not be the same size, as is demonstrated in "Fifth Grade Banner." An interesting approach was used for the Peruvian mural, with the individual pieces well arranged and stitched on a large background. Stimulating projects made up of individual pieces could be "Birds We Never Saw," or "Birds of our State," "Fish That Never Swam," "Flowers as Seen by a Bird," "Wildflowers We Saw," "Imaginary Bugs and Butterflies." Ribbon, tape, or colorful felt strips can be used over the joints to separate the pieces.

THE FIFTH GRADE BANNER. This gay banner, over six feet in length is a good example of how individual pieces can be mounted together, as they were by Irene Preston Miller, the children's teacher, to form a colorful whole. It was the children's first attempt at stitchery. The burlap pieces are joined with multicolor strips of felt. Mrs. Miller relates that what she enjoys most about the banner is the many interpretations of the sun, although no mention had been made of the sun in the class! The banner is displayed at the Carrie E. Tompkins school in Croton-on-Hudson. (Photograph by Michael Miller.)

NOAH'S ARK. "Noah's Ark" is a particularly delightful freehand mural worked by many boys and girls in Mrs. Bryant's fifth grade class in the Van Ness Elementary Public School, Washington, D.C.

The children stitched whenever they had a free period, a few of them at a time. They were encouraged to use their imagination and create freely; one of the girls chalked in what her classmates had in mind. They did not start at one end and work across; they stitched wherever they felt their contribution to the whole should be. They were not helped in any way by the teachers, the only request being that each child should finish the animal or the detail he had started. Note the Bible being carried on board, and to me the most amusing touch of all, the two skunks in a cage on a raft at the back of the ark! One child was determined to have skunks in the ark, the others objected, hence the compromise. As they stitched, the children made up a delightful song about Noah and the Ark in the tradition of the spirituals of the South: "Oh, Noah, He said, there's gonna be a floody, floody . . ." Hearing the children singing their song with appropriate gestures is something I shall never forget.

The wide piece, 14 by 3 feet, shows a great deal of spontaneity. It is a remarkable example of the creative genius in children. (Photograph by Colonel Martin D. McAllister.)

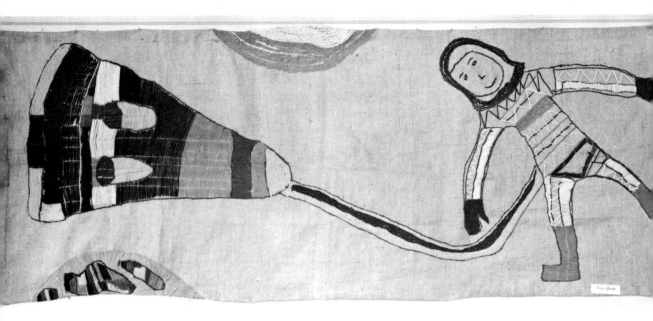

MAN IN SPACE. The man at the end of the capsule's line conveys an amazing sense of weightlessness and floating in space. Worked by a number of sixth-grade boys and girls in the Watkins Elementary Public School, Washington, D.C., the piece is entirely the result of the children's imaginative interpretation of what they had watched on television: an astronaut walking in space. (Photograph by Colonel Martin D. McAllister.)

Detail of a wall hanging 12 feet wide, SPORTS AROUND THE WORLD, conceived by sixth-grade boys at Sunny Brae Avenue School, Canoga Park, California.

The boys' teacher, William Cahill Johnson, writes: "This figure portrays a native of the New Hebrides jumping from a tower with vines tied to his ankles. One of the boys in my class had seen this type of native sport on a television program. The idea is to fall in such a way that the head just misses the ground. It is a rather unusual sport which appealed to this one lad." The action is really lived. The excellent effect shows how expert 11-year-old boys can be when they catch their teacher's enthusiasm. In the same class the girls worked on a mural showing girls in different costumes in various parts of the world. (Photograph by Fred Figgins.)

When a mural is planned by a group and the subject matter chosen, possible background materials should be discussed. Drapery yardage may furnish ideas. Coarse linens are beautiful and desirable but costly. Burlap is the least expensive, comes in many beautiful colors, and has interesting texture; get the best quality. It can be spray-starched on the back to give it body and discourage puckering. Several light coats work better than one heavy application, as the color of burlap sometimes runs when wet.

The approximate size of the mural should be decided, keeping in mind that this will be in part determined by materials available. Burlap for instance comes in 40-inch width. If the mural is made of one large piece, curved bag needles are indispensable when working in the middle, to avoid having to work around the piece (see page 165).

One of many approaches is to secure on the wall a piece of paper the size and approximate color of the projected mural. This will provide a working surface with a feeling for scale and placement. When each child has decided what his part will be, in an atmosphere hopefully charged with excitement, he can draw and color the outline of his contribution to the whole on a separate piece of paper, using crayons the color of the yarns available, avoiding detail, and keeping in mind that stitches rather than crayon or paint will express his thought. If the cloth background is colored, it is useful, though not essential, to work on paper of the same color. The children should cut out their own shapes, in clean-cut lines, then lay them on the paper mural, which at this point can be laid flat on a table so that the pieces can be moved around freely for the best arrangement. This is an opportunity for discussion of balance, of relative sizes and possible overlaps, of how to fill the space. The foreground and background can be planned. When the general placement is agreed upon, each shape should be pinned in place on the cloth so that the piece as a whole can be viewed from a distance and discussed. Changes are apt to be made at this stage. Stitches and yarns to be used can be thought of in better perspective, yarns can be actually pinned up for color values and texture effect.

When the group is satisfied, each child can transfer his shape to the cloth, either freehand with chalk or by tracing around his cut shape. A fine nylon-tip pen can be used over the chalk lines. A minimum of lines should be drawn; all details should be stitched freehand. When real excitement is there, stitches will take on a special, unique quality that no predrawn piece can ever achieve.

Shapes can be first outlined with a quick Running or Darning Stitch with one or two threads picked up, or with Double Running Stitch. These can be Whipped or Threaded to provide a heavier line. Further stressing of the line can be achieved with two or three rows close together. Besides Outline Stitch, many stitches can be used to outline shapes and to fill them. The experience of working on the cloth will bring about changes and ideas such as color distribution, more or less of one color, the need for accents. Each child should feel the importance of his contribution to the whole and the importance of the other contributors. Pride in the group accomplishment is very important. The intensity of the stimulation will carry through and find expression. It is an experience the children never forget.

In schools, murals can become a permanent decoration for classrooms, hallways, library, or dining hall. The examples given were chosen from many because each one illustrates a different approach and response to group work in different parts of the country.

IV. Children with Special Needs

THE PHYSICALLY HANDICAPPED—
THE MENTALLY RETARDED

"To teach is to love." Of no group is this truer than of those who work with children who have problems, whether these be physical, mental, or both. I make no claim to medical or technical knowledge as regards these children. I want to help all children to have the rewarding experience and the joy that come from creating something with their hands. The following pages were written in the hope that the suggestions and examples given will be helpful to the mothers and teachers of children who have difficulties.

The examples shown, identified by the initials NWCR, were worked at the Northwest Center for Retarded, in Seattle, Washington, with the cooperation of teachers Linda Moon in charge of art projects, Naomi Miller, Ann Eickhoff, and Betty Probert. The other examples were worked at Pacific Prevocational School in Seattle, in the classes of Doris Lough and Susan Freeman.

Stitchery is a craft which can be used successfully in the case of many handicapped children, regardless of the nature of the handicap or the child's mental age, and without expensive equipment. It can be used in homes as well as in schools. It is an activity which leads to self-esteem, self-help, one in which the special child finds it easier to identify himself as an individual, with other children, and with the home: "I'm sewing."

There is something about stitchery which reaches deeply into children's minds and emotions. Many of us have experienced the pleasure of handling skeins and balls of beautiful colored yarns of all types. Perhaps it is the colors, the feel of the textile, or the DOING of something personal, something somewhat grown-up and permanent, that brings special joy and a feeling of comfort to children.

Of all children, those who are handicapped have the greatest need for creative expression. Professor William C. Ward, Jr. has found that "Creativity is not at all related to intelligence, as measured with standard tests." Stitchery is an activity which enables the handicapped to reach a degree of self-expression, bringing the NEEDED EMOTIONAL SATISFACTION OF ACCOMPLISHMENT.

One of the most valuable therapeutic results is the means it provides for the child to communicate. It is easier for some children to communicate through their hands. Description in words is often too hard. Some children for instance, are not able to talk about their homes. Others cannot describe in words how they come to school, giving the impression that they do not observe or have no recollection. Yet some of them can create a detailed description of the experience on hardware cloth, canvas, or burlap, when given the opportunity to tell their story in their own way. This reliving of an experience can be found in recognizable shapes or it can be in the deliberate choice of specific colors. The results can be revealing and show character; they can be a bridge towards communication. Some children use stitchery to tell a story, or to make precise designs — some of them beautiful — while others enjoy the manipulation with no attempt at expression. All are valuable experiences.

The nature of the handicap and the rate of progress vary so much with the special problem of each child that no attempt has been made at classification by physical or mental age. Mothers and teachers can adapt the suggestions to the handicap of the child, encouraging him to stretch to the utmost his physical and mental potential.

Illustrations in this section were selected to show a variety of responses and the captions were written to suggest areas of experimentation. The stages described at the preschool level for the child who is not handicapped can be tried with the handicapped child who will respond at his own level. He, too, learns by DOING, but unlike the average child, he may need additional help, such as working with him at a slower pace, repeating directions as often as necessary, not expecting too much, and accepting wholeheartedly what the child produces.

Some children need help to the point of actually holding their hands and going through the motions with them over and over again. Some cannot originate an idea but can work with stitches, on lines drawn for them. Others will repeat the same symbol over and over again because it does not require an effort. There should be enough encouragement, not too much, not doing the child's work for him but urging him on in an unpressured atmosphere. It takes infinite patience, flexibility, and imagination. What is important is the process of learning, not necessarily the result.

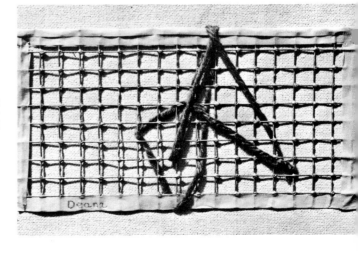

Deana is severely retarded. She has a very short attention span. This piece meant a great effort for her. The teacher at NWCR had to hold her hand but she showed that she enjoyed the DOING.

PREPARATION AND START

Everything should be prepared ahead of time to make the experience inviting, to avoid restrictions and frustrations. The needs of the child and his physical and mental age determine what materials to use. Remember what was said on page 6 about the average child: be ready for action when he is ready to start.

Hardware cloth, with edges well protected with masking tape, is good for beginners at any age (see page 154). Because the hardware cloth is rigid, it provides a solid base upon which to develop muscular control. Progress from 1/2-inch mesh to 1/4-inch and then to 1/8-inch; from small pieces, such as 5 by 8 inches for small hands, to larger pieces.

At all stages use yarn that will go through the mesh easily, all-cotton rug yarn (see page 163) rather than wool or rayon mixtures. Use single strands, not stranded cottons because these pull unevenly. The choice of colors should be limited at the beginning and increased slowly. Choices can bring confusion. Some children can be taught to measure the yarn, perhaps using the width of the table as a yardstick, and to cut the desired length.

The fear of giving a sharp needle to a child who might hurt himself or others has frequently prevented the use of the stitchery experience. At first needles are not needed; instead, harden the ends of the yarn as described on page 166. When a child can be given a needle, start with the large tapestry size 14, which goes easily through 1/4-inch mesh. He is not apt to have difficulties with it: the point is not sharp and if it is dropped, it is easy to see. If it is properly anchored (see page 18) there is little chance of his losing it. Be sure to have the right size for the material used; always choose a needle as large as possible but one which will slip easily through the mesh when threaded with appropriate yarn.

Robert's teacher at the NWCR says about him: "He had shown no interest in manual work; he didn't draw or paint when the others did. This 12 by 6 piece of 1/4-inch hardware cloth attracted him and was a real challenge to him. He started by himself and covered the piece in about four sessions, using a different color each time. It was the longest attention span he had ever shown. This piece motivated Robert and helped him a great deal. From then on he showed interest in crafts, painting, drawing and was very pleased with himself. He is a hyperactive boy with brain damage. This activity helped him to settle his emotional frustrations."

At NWCR, John, who has brain damage, explored with obvious pleasure on a piece of wire mesh 13 by 9 inches, using pearl cotton size 3 in a variety of colors. He completed it in one period. The impression made must have been vivid, as John, seeing me again after an interval of almost a year, smiled, thought, then said one word: "Sewing." It meant recollection and communication, which was remarkable as he had seen me only four times.

To vary the experience, children could be given fiber-glass screening which can be bound with masking tape. Some children who have made a drawing on paper can learn to transfer it to the fiberglass screening by placing the screening over their drawing, outlining shapes on the mesh and filling them, keeping the original drawing as a guide for detail. The taut yet supple mesh gives them a feeling of security. They discover the joy of a permanent picture with texture. It is a very useful experience, both tactual and mental.

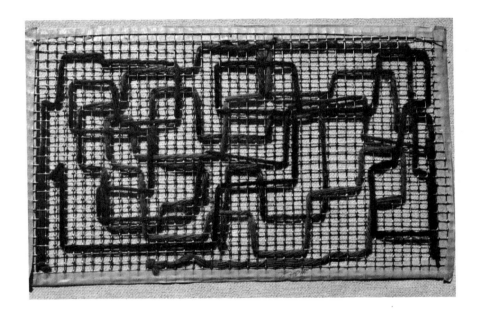

This was Joel's first experience with stitchery. When he was given the 8- by 12-inch piece of $\frac{1}{4}$-inch hardware cloth and lengths of cotton rug yarn with ends hardened, there was no reaction — he just held the piece. As his teacher was busy with other children, I tied a length of yarn at the center of the bottom edge, went over and under 2 or 3 mesh and handed it to Joel. The boy took it eagerly and very quickly made a design, repeating a definite pattern, creating a rhythm through repetition. He used a new color every time he ran out of yarn, tying the new yarn very neatly himself, until the area was covered. I was elated with the result and went over to his teacher to tell her about the experience. When I came back to Joel, he was in the process of neatly, quickly, almost angrily un-

doing everything he had done, and my heart sank. I had wanted everyone to admire the piece and I wanted to take a photograph of it.

Fortunately, I did not question him. He was very absorbed and seemed to have a definite idea in mind. When every last stitch was ripped off, Joel started again in exactly the same spot, tying the yarn very neatly and leaving no tail end. Then he proceeded to repeat almost exactly the first design. When he was through, he handed it to me with a very satisfied look on his face. It was then I realized that the first attempt was spoiled for him because I had had a part in it and, most of all, I had left an untidy inch or so of trailing yarn at the beginning. Joel wanted all of it to be his, HIS doing, and perfect; it was. (NWCR)

Barbara is severely retarded yet stitchery became a happy experience for her. The work had to be planned for her because she was either unable to originate an idea or unable to translate her thought to the burlap. Sitting by her side, the teacher drew a flower on the burlap, a shape so simple that Barbara could understand it. After that she needed little help; she worked precisely and fast, choosing her own colors. It is actually an excellent piece of work for any child. Working with a needle may open the way to a useful occupation for Barbara. (NWCR)

Barbara's flower shape gave Joel the idea he was waiting for as he fingered a piece of starched burlap, looking bored. It was the stimulation he needed to start something of his own. He worked fast, with intensity, filling the space completely, and showing a real sense of design. He shows great promise in art. His speech is severely impaired and communication is difficult. Stitchery gives him great pleasure. It is for him a means of expression. (NWCR)

Norma, another child in the same group, filled the space with haphazard stitches with no special meaning, just enjoying doing something with cloth and yarns. Although the result may appear to be disappointing, what is important is the benefit the child derived from a new experience. This stage is one most children go through. The rate of progress is slower for some than for others. (NWCR)

As control and finger dexterity are acquired, vary the experience. Go from hardware cloth to large mesh lino weave canvas and then to monocanvas, or fiberglass screening, gradually leading up to an open weave cloth such as burlap. Vary the size, color,and texture. As each step is mastered, progress is made; there is growth.

Handicapped children respond particularly to cloth stretched on LIGHT frames (see page 162), rather than holding unmounted cloth. It makes a great deal of difference. Start with small sizes, 6 by 10 inches for the very young child, then 8 by 10, increasing to 10 by 12. I have found that groups such as Scouts, Campfire Girls and other organizations looking for a project are happy to make simple frames for these children. If frames are not possible, use hoops with a screw. Failing these, starch the material so that it is not limp (see page 160).

Children in bed or wheelchairs find lap frames useful. Those who can use only one hand can use table frames which are clamped to the edge of a table or wheelchair. Some children require special equipment which has to be made to fit the need. This is an area in which an imaginative parent, teacher, or physical therapist can be very helpful.

The attention span is apt to be short, although it is amazing to see the deep concentration, the extended length of the attention span and the patience many of these children bring to the stitchery experience. At home it seems to establish a special kind of rapport with the mother, particularly when she is "sewing" at the same time. I have watched retarded children discover the joy and SECURITY of going over and under the hardware cloth or lino weave canvas mesh in regular patterns. It is the same joy experienced by the normal child. I find it very moving.

Some children show progress from one step to the next; many are not capable of a sustained effort; others, who perhaps did good work on their first attempt, will seem to regress. The teachers at the Northwest Center for Retarded tell me that this happens fairly frequently although they are not always aware of what brought on the regression. When this happens, and the child no longer shows interest, it is best to stop the specific activity and change to another one, trying again at a later time with new stimulation.

It is not necessary to teach stitches until a specific need occurs. If the child feels the need, he will absorb the knowledge. A simple Running Stitch can be made to express almost anything by the use of repetition and by varying direction and angle, color and texture. ONE SHOULD NOT AIM AT PERFECTION. Strangely, many of these children ARE perfectionists and delight in the repetition of small even stitches, undoing and redoing until they feel satisfied. This trait can be developed into valuable skills with which they can at least partially support themselves when the need arises. For instance, if heavy yarns are used, lino weave canvas can be completely covered with stitches and made into practical articles such as rugs, bags, and cushions.

Encourage the child to finish what he has started so that he will experience the satisfaction of a completed project. For this reason it is best, at first, to plan a project that will only take one or two sessions to finish.

Whenever possible, let the decorated cloth be made into something the child can use or which can become a present for others: tote bag, book covers, pictures on the wall, pot holders, cushions. Some projects such as sewing on buttons, perhaps for the eyes of a self-portrait, can lead them to sewing buttons on their own clothes.

At Pacific Prevocational School, Seattle, Washington, Doris Lough teaches art to boys and girls academically retarded. She has a remarkable ability to reach these children and communicate with them. Through their art work she encourages them to think and to express themselves.

These self-portraits by Ken and Linda are fresh and free. Ken is at the left, and Linda at the right. The children loved working on burlap stretched over frames.

Some of Susan Freeman's pupils at the Pacific Prevocational School are severely mentally retarded. Sharon, who is not able to communicate with words, made this stitchery of "Me and my friend." Turquoise burlap was stretched on one of the frames made by a group of Girl Scouts. It made the stitching easier and more satisfying.

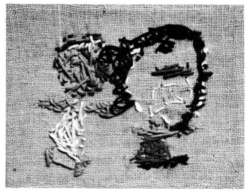

"How do you come to school?" It was not possible for severely retarded Victor in Susan Freeman's class to describe this everyday occurrence; he looked as if he had observed nothing. Yet when he was given a piece of 1/4-inch hardware cloth, he quickly made a picture of the school service car which brought him to school, correctly choosing the colors of the car, three shades of blue with black. He was triumphant; he had in his own way answered the question. He experienced the ineffable joy of finding a way to communicate with another human being. (Pacific Prevocational School.)

It is particularly important to display the work suitably and to refer to it often to reassure the child that he has done something good, something that is admired and brings praise. It builds up a feeling of security through achievement and stimulates him into making the effort again. It gives him the joy of accomplishment, emotional satisfaction, and helps him to grow.

Handicapped children are by no means entirely on the receiving end. Their needs stimulate our thinking. I owe to these children one of the most exciting discoveries of my life, the process of anchoring a needle (see page 18). This process has no doubt been discovered before, but I had never heard of it. I had been attending a conference on recreation for the retarded at the University of Washington and was urging a group of teachers to try stitchery as a means of expression. Two of the teachers remarked that they had tried it but found that they could not cope with 15 children unthreading their 15 needles every time they took a stitch — a "simple" but shattering problem. The thought that the fruitful experience of stitchery must be denied to these children for a mechanical reason kept me awake for many hours.

The joy of finding the solution has not left me. As one child so aptly put it, "It's magic," a magic many can learn. Soon after this discovery I was watching a retarded woman in her thirties who found great satisfaction and emotional relief in stitchery. Her work had a primitive quality which made it very appealing. However, every few stitches the needle would pull out and the resulting irritation and frustration were very apparent. She found threading the needle difficult and an unwelcome interruption. I showed her how to anchor the needle. This took time but she did learn to do this herself and the joy in her face was just as great as in John's, on page 19. Through the needs of handicapped children all children are benefiting.

THE LEFT-HANDED CHILD

While being left-handed is not strictly speaking a physical handicap, it does involve problems, if only because most instructions are written for right-handed people. I was not fully aware of the prevalence of this problem until I came across many left-handed children in schools.

The solution was given to me by a left-handed person who was using diagrams in my earlier book, *The Stitches of Creative Embroidery,* with the book turned around, reading the letters upside down. Take the diagram shown here for instance (same as Figure 8 on page 56). The letters read, from RIGHT TO LEFT, AB CD E. Turn the book around. The letters are upside down and read from LEFT TO RIGHT, AB CD E. If the child is too young to read diagrams, let the adult follow it, using his left hand. It is amazing how easy it becomes; the child can then watch and imitate. As soon as a child can recognize letters, he can follow diagrams. If need be, the letters can be penciled in, right side up, as was done in the upside-down diagram in smaller letters. Whenever the directions read — for example — right to left, substitute left to right, and so forth.

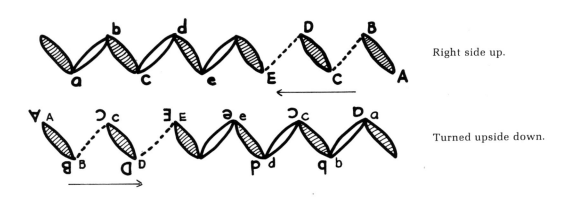

Right side up.

Turned upside down.

151

Cathie is blind and severely retarded. This was her first "sewing" experience. Her enjoyment was evident. She was able to go in and out of the lino-weave canvas, using rug yarns in cotton and wool, chenille yarn, and a silk cord, each with one end hardened. Although varied textures were given to her, she did not seem aware of the difference. In time she may be able to distinguish wool from cotton and silk, and to understand such concepts as front and back, over and under. (NWCR)

THE BLIND CHILD

There are a number of areas where children with special needs can profitably use the experience of stitchery. Blind children, with their touch sensitivity, can start with hardware cloth and lino weave rug canvas (see pages 154-156). Yarns in a variety of textures can be tried, textured areas can be created. Besides cotton rug yarns, these children enjoy the softness of chenille yarns, which are often used by hand weavers (Lily Mills Company, Shelby, North Carolina, manufactures them in many colors). Chenille works best with ends hardened rather than with needles (see page 166). There is also variety in the feeling of jute, mohair, raffia.

EMOTIONALLY OR SOCIALLY MALADJUSTED CHILDREN

Another field to explore is that of children who are emotionally or socially maladjusted. Working at their own level, many find relief in working off some of their tensions and frustrations through the medium of stitchery. An opportunity to express themselves creatively can be invaluable to them.

PRESCHOOL ENRICHMENT PROGRAMS

Children in preschool enrichment programs for the culturally and economically disadvantaged benefit from the experience of stitchery. There are many programs such as Head Start, and a number of similar privately operated groups working with the very young disadvantaged. Stitchery is a real help towards these children's development. Many of them have never seen a mother sewing. Besides the emotional deprivation, they have no concept of

Vincent, Wade, and Charlene, with Rosemary Enthoven, at Junior Village, Washington, D.C., intent on their first stitchery.

many basic related words usually learned at home as a matter of course. When a 4-year-old who had never known home life was introduced to the experience of "sewing" for the first time, he looked puzzled and rubbed his arm when the word "needle" was used.

THE ACADEMICALLY GIFTED CHILD

Another child who often needs help is the academically talented child. A great deal of attention is now given to developing ways of helping the academic underachiever. Some thought should be directed toward the child who excels in intellectual skills but finds it difficult to express himself creatively with materials that involve the use of his hands. He, too, experiences frustrations. In order to become a well-rounded person he must learn to face and solve problems that are of a different nature. He should learn to translate his thoughts and feelings through appropriate manual skills. Stitchery may provide a challenge towards artistic expression, a field that may be new to him, not based upon his highly developed verbal achievements.

It is my hope that stitchery will be used towards the development of ALL children, that this book will open new doors for them and help them to experience the joy of expressing themselves creatively.

V. Suggested Materials

HARDWARE CLOTH, FIBERGLASS SCREENING, AND PERFORATED ALUMINUM

Hardware cloth is a metal mesh which comes in $1/8$-, $1/4$-, $1/2$-inch mesh. Fiberglass is used for window screens. There are also metal screenings and varieties of perforated aluminum. Obtainable in hardware stores or lumber yards, these materials are inexpensive and come in various widths. One $1/4$-yard of 18-inch width will make three 6-by-9 pieces. Cut hardware cloth with tin snips or heavy scissors; fiberglass and perforated aluminum sheets with kitchen scissors. Cover the edges with colorful vinyl, plastic, or masking tape to protect the child from sharp points, and in the case of fiberglass to prevent ravelling. (See illustrations on pages 13, 8, 145, 9.)

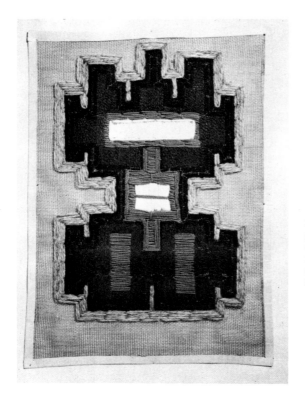

Design on fiberglass. Byron, age 10, has heard a great deal about design at home. He likes to draw architectural subjects and felt that the mesh called for a geometric design which unfolded as he went along. It was his first experience with yarn and needle.

CANVAS

Canvas is obtainable in needlework shops and department stores; it is referred to as so many mesh to the inch. Avoid canvas with holes that are too small, preferably not more than 10 to the inch. For young children choose 3, 4, or 5 holes to the inch — the younger the child, the larger the holes. Canvas comes in several widths, in white, ecru, and yellow.

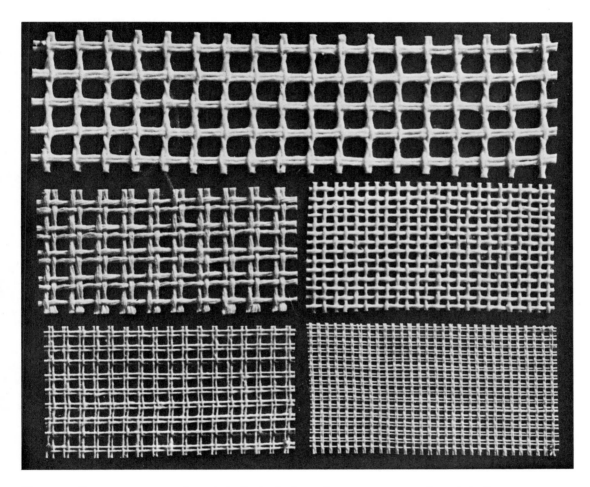

First row: lino-weave canvas, 3 mesh to the inch. Second row: rug canvas, 5 mesh to the inch; monocanvas, 10 mesh to the inch. Third row: Cross Stitch canvas, 7 mesh to the inch; penelope canvas, 10 mesh to the inch.

There are two general types: single thread and double thread. The single-thread canvas — monocanvas — has one thread crossing one other, making regular squares. Children often prefer monocanvas. There are several kinds of double-thread canvas: Cross-Stitch and rug canvas have two threads crossing two others, evenly spaced. Another kind, penelope canvas, has two close vertical threads crossing two not-so-close horizontal threads.

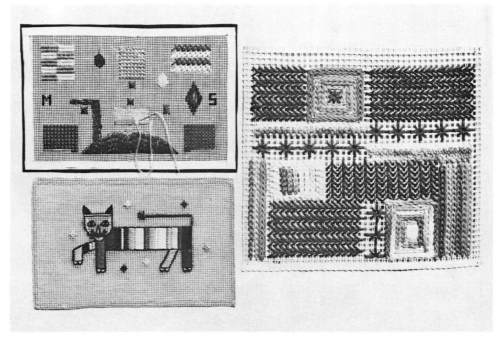

Left, top: Mary S., age 13, learned stitches and color combinations on a piece of mono-canvas. It ended up as a sampler. Right: sampler on rug canvas, 4 mesh to the inch. Theresa, age 10, first planned her design with cut papers in the colors of her blue, orange, red, and variegated pink yarns. She was intrigued with the precision of the medium and commented: "This is wonderful. You can't make a mistake!" Left, bottom: cat, on penelope canvas, by the author.

The best canvas for preschool children, for children with manipulative problems, or for blind children, is a fairly rigid rug canvas known by a variety of names. It is technically a lino-weave canvas made up of two pairs of threads crossing each other, forming squares. The pairs of horizontal threads, from selvedge to selvedge, are parallel and stuck together. The pairs of vertical threads are twisted around the horizontal threads and also stuck together. This canvas is usually 40 inches wide, with 3 or 4 holes (mesh) to the inch. It does not ravel, so that the edges do not have to be bound, which is helpful to the teacher in a class with many children. A needle is not necessary when the tip of the yarn is hardened with glue.

A 13-year-old retarded boy at the Pacific Prevocational School in Seattle created his own design on lino-weave canvas, without any special guidance. He loved the process and was the first child to work a row with diagonal stitches, at the bottom edge.

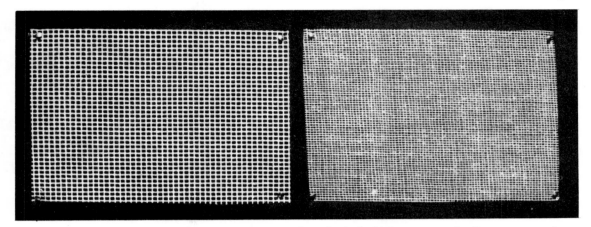

Left: nylon crinoline, approximately 20 mesh to the inch. Right: cotton crinoline.

CRINOLINE

Crinoline, made of nylon or cotton, is a stiffened open-weave fabric used for interlining. The best type to use is nylon crinoline — sometimes referred to as nylon mesh — a fine square-mesh material, about 20 squares to the inch, usually 44 inches wide. It is inexpensive, very transparent, and most suitable for children's stitcheries, stapled over paper. It is wonderful for transferring designs (see page 163). Nylon net is too light for the purpose. Cotton crinoline, better known than nylon, can be used for the same purpose, although not quite as suitable; this is not to be confused with buckram, which is much stiffer and not at all suitable.

PAPER: RUBBERIZED AND PLASTICIZED

Paper for children's stitcheries should be firm yet flexible, so that it will not tear while stitching. Ordinary drawing or construction papers can be used; however, these are apt to tear, which is discouraging. A good quality rubberized and plastic-coated shelf-lining paper, such as Marvellon, is stronger than regular paper. The rubberized treatment gives flexibility, making it more resistant to tearing. Be sure it is the non-adhesive kind, which is available in rolls as narrow as 12 inches — sometimes with one edge scalloped — with the rubberized and plasticized side colored. The under side has a pleasing texture due to a small amount of color showing through. That is the side to use. If the child should want to use the color side, a bright, plain color is best; patterns would be distracting for the beginner and defeat the purpose.

CLOTH

Cloth for children's stitcheries should be easy to pierce with a tapestry needle, which has a blunt point. Avoid tightly woven uninspiring materials

First row: even weave linen; rough textured linen. Second row: two-over-two linen; two-over-two cotton monk's cloth. Third row: cotton homespun; heavy cotton homespun. Bottom: burlap.

At the Acomita Day School in New Mexico, 9-year-old Carmen made a remarkable job of the regular, colorful design on the bag because she could follow easily the definite weave of the burlap.

such as sheeting and muslin. The cloth should be firm enough so that it will not pucker: it should have body and yet be flexible. A heavy open-weave linen (not over 20 threads to the inch, preferably less) would be ideal. However, this may be too expensive for regular use by children and should be reserved for something special.

The best quality burlap, often referred to as washable burlap, is very suitable as long as it is stiffened or held taut in a frame or hoop (see pages 160-162). It has a pleasing texture and comes in many colors. Cream or off white make a good background. Natural is very good if it is not too dark. Colors are also good; however, they fade in time and sometimes run if wet. The great advantage of burlap is that it is inexpensive and easily available.

For beginners, pieces could be 9 by 10 inches. As the child grows older, try larger pieces, vary the size and the proportions; 18 by 18 inches provides a good margin for mounting over a large frame.

Two-over-two monk's cloth, off white, is good. This is a cotton basketweave material with two threads for warp and two for weft. It is particularly useful for learning the mechanics of stitches and for stitch samplers. Hopsacking and cotton homespun, regular or heavy, are all suitable; spray-starch the back for added body (see page 160). Look at drapery and upholstery remnants for different and unusual textures. Striped or checkered material, if not tightly woven, can provide a change, using the lines as a guide or for part of a design. One child used large checks for a "Jack and Jill Went Up the Hill" picture.

Although felt is sometimes suggested, it is hard to pull the needle and thread through the tight texture. When too much physical effort has to be made, the joy of stitching is lost.

Whatever cloth you use, unless it is stretched over a frame, run a strip of 1/4-inch masking tape around the back or a 1/2-inch tape over the edge to prevent raveling. A zigzag stitch on the machine or a thin line of Elmer's glue on the edge of the back will also prevent raveling.

HOLDING THE CLOTH TAUT

It is often difficult and frustrating for children (and adults too!) to keep limp material from puckering as they stitch. Several methods can be used to prevent the problem from arising. The material can be held taut in a frame or in a hoop. When it is impractical to provide frames or hoops for a group of children, stiffen the cloth as described below.

Preschool children work best with the cloth stretched in a small hoop. School-age children do their best work when the material is stretched on a lightweight frame, because it gives them a feeling for all-over design. It makes stitches such as knots and couching easier to do well. It also makes possible the use of unusual materials such as various coarse nets. Some children like the feel of the material directly in their hands. This need not create a problem if the material has been given sufficient body. If possible, vary the method used and see which one brings the best results.

STIFFENING THE CLOTH

The quickest and easiest way to stiffen cloth such as burlap is to use a pressure can of spray starch. Spray two or three light coats on one side of the material, ironing between coats with a warm (not hot) iron, or spray one heavy coat and, if possible, iron it dry. A paper towel or a cloth over the material prevents the iron from sticking. The aim is to give enough body to the cloth so that it will not pucker when stitched, and yet not be too rigid. The starched side should be treated as the back of the stitchery.

A less expensive but also satisfactory way is to dilute liquid starch concentrate with water, half and half, and either spray or paint the back with a brush. When many pieces have to be prepared, as in a class room, the quickest way is to pour a half water, half starch concentrate solution on a cookie tray and dip the back of each piece on top of the solution, rubbing off the excess to keep the material from becoming too stiff. On large pieces, such as murals, a spray-can or large brush should be used.

If you are dealing with a very flimsy material and yet want to use it because of a special texture or color, you will find that ironing the lightest weight of non-woven interlining on the back — the kind that sticks when

Back of the mountain goat pictured on page 85. The goat was worked out with paper and scissors. The outline was transferred to the lightest weight of non-woven interlining, the type which sticks to cloth when pressed with a hot iron. Applied to the burlap, this did two things: it gave body to the burlap so that a frame was not needed; it also gave a precise guide line on the back for the outline of the goat. This method gives freedom to change as the work proceeds since there are no lines on the front.

ironed on — gives good results. It comes in several weights. Be sure it is the lightest weight and non-woven as the woven type is harder to stitch. A pointed needle, such as crewel or embroidery No. 1, makes the work easier. This would be too expensive for school use but might fill a need for home use. I used this method on the looped stitchery, shown on page 85, because I wanted a definite outline for the goat and did not want to draw on the dark blue burlap. I drew it reversed on the light interlining and ironed it on. The rest was stitched freehand.

HOOPS

A hoop is particularly suited to the preschool child. It makes changes of cloth quick and easy, an essential feature at that age. Be sure that the hoop is made of light wood and that it is tightened with a screw, not with a spring, which pops off. The screw allows for adjustment to the thickness of the material and makes a really tight surface possible. The best size for preschool children is 6 inches in diameter. Sewing machine companies often stock them. Because this type of hoop is round and the edge narrow, it can be grasped and held easily by a small hand. A piece of cloth 9 by 9 inches is sufficient for a 6-inch hoop. Older children may enjoy an 8-inch hoop. There are also lap hoops, table hoops, and standing hoops.

Hoops are apt to leave a mark on fabrics and to crush stitches that are already made. This is not a problem for the preschool child. For myself, I overcome this crushing of the fabric by placing a discarded piece of cloth under my stitchery material and running a row of machine basting in a circle about half an inch inside the circle where the hoop will be placed, stitching both pieces of material together. Then I place the inside hoop under both cloths, the outside hoop over both cloths, and carefully lift the top cloth over the outside hoop. The two hoops should be directly over each other, one inside the other, with the under-cloth between. Before I tighten the screw, I make a slit in the center of the under cloth. I then tighten the screw and stretch the cloths. When both the cloths are taut, I slide my scissors in the slit and cut off the under cloth to within half an inch of the circle of basting stitches. My stitchery material is taut and yet no hoop is crushing my work. When the work is done, I release the screw and take out the basting.

Hoops and frames. One 8-inch lap hoop with burlap, two 6-inch and one 9-inch hoop. Two 10- by 14-inch frames, one shown with burlap, ready to hang.

FRAMES

Although stitchery frames adjustable to various sizes are commercially available, they are heavy and not suitable for the average child. It is easy and inexpensive to make light frames for children. Measure the material you plan to use, allowing an inch extra on all sides for turning back over the edge of the frame. From a hardware store or a lumber yard, get ³/₄-inch flat screen molding, preferably pine wood, which is easier to staple. It is sold by the foot for a few cents. For a child 6 to 8 years old you might cut two pieces 10 or 12 inches long (AB and CD on the diagram), then two pieces 9 or 10 inches long, EF and GH. For older children try larger sizes, such as 12 by 16 inches, or vary the proportions, for instance, 12 by 18, 10 by 18. Assemble by first cementing the joints either with an electric glue gun, or with contact cement or Elmer's glue. It helps if you pull the edges together with two staples on the front and on the back. Reinforce the joints with angles of stiff cardboard or cardboard-backed vinyl, cemented or glued over the joints for a tight seal. For extra strength, angles can be cemented or glued over the front as well as the back. This is important when making frames for children with handicaps. Another way to reinforce the joints is by use of Scotch strapping tape, going around over the edges in both directions. Since the stitchery is meant to remain framed and a new frame is used each time, it does not need to be quite as strong as a frame that is used many times; it should, however, be sufficiently well-made so that it will not come apart in use. I like to make several frames at one time. An inexpensive, ready-made picture frame can be used, provided it is light in weight, fairly flat, and narrow so that it will be easy to grasp. Physical tension is apt to slow the flow of a child's enthusiasm.

Place the cloth over the frame, turning the edges to the back, and staple in place on the back with a staple gun, stretching the cloth as you staple it. If the material is very loose, back it with a strip of masking tape on the edges, which will give strength to hold the staples. If you have no staples, use thumbtacks but cover them with masking tape so they won't pop off.

Frames can also be made from pieces of heavy cardboard by cutting out the center, leaving an inch-wide frame; the material is fastened with masking tape on the back. Although these are not as strong as wooden frames, they

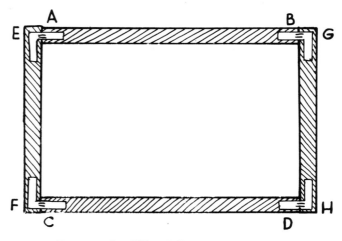

Frame made of ³/₄-inch flat screen molding.
For this molding use ⁴/₁₆-inch staples.

can be adequate if not too large. Curt's fish stitchery (see page 75) was made in such a frame. It would not be suitable for handicapped children.

Making frames for children is worth the trouble; it stimulates them to do their best and the results are more pleasing to them, with the added satisfaction of being able to hang the piece immediately by adding a screw eye to each side with a string between. It is a good project for fathers and grandfathers!

TRANSFERRING A DESIGN

Children should be encouraged to work out their ideas with needle and thread directly on the cloth. There is a freshness of expression that is lost when a design is transferred. If at the start they feel the need of a definite outline, let them draw freehand on the cloth with a sharpened piece of chalk which can be easily brushed off. If freehand drawing does not seem possible, the next best thing is for children to draw the needed shapes on drawing paper, cut out the shapes, place them on the material, and pin them down. This is a good way as it allows changes and freedom in placement. They can then trace around the shapes with chalk or with a fine nylon tip type of pen with indelible ink the color of the yarns.

Transferring a design to cloth has been a problem as the usual methods, such as dressmaker's carbon, wax crayon tracings ironed on, transferring against a sunny window, are not always satisfactory. I worked out a solution to the problem with the use of a new material, nylon crinoline, sometimes referred to as nylon mesh, (see page 157), which works wonderfully with children — and adults too! Nylon crinoline is not the same thing as nylon net which is too open for the purpose and not rigid enough. It is inexpensive and the same piece can be used many times for the same or different designs. It is as transparent as layout paper. If nylon crinoline is not obtainable, it is possible to use cotton crinoline. To transfer, place the design on a hard surface. Lay a piece of nylon crinoline over it; secure the crinoline to the design with masking tape or thumbtacks. With a hard nylon-tip pen, trace the design right on the crinoline, gently, so that the ink will not go through. A hard tipped pen must be used; felt pens are too soft and thick. A laundry marking pen or a hard water-proof pencil can be used. Next, lay the crinoline over the well-pressed cloth, on a hard surface, center well, and secure them together with masking tape or thumb-tacks. Using the same type of pen, preferably with ink close to the color of the yarns (in case the lines are not covered with stitches) or well sharpened color pencils, go over the lines pressing HARD. Test first to see how hard. The design will be transferred to the cloth. When you remove the crinoline, you may need to go lightly over some of the lines, depending on the texture of the material. This works well even on coarse textured materials such as burlap on which it is difficult to transfer by any other method. If the material is dark, use a hard white or light-yellow pencil. If the material is to be washed or blocked with water, indelible ink or pencils must be used or else the ink will run.

YARNS

For the preschool child and often through the second grade, also for children who have manipulative difficulties, cotton yarns are easiest to manage because wool tends to snarl and make the process of pulling discouraging.

Some cotton yarns are mixed with spun rayon; unless the rayon content is a very small percentage, avoid these yarns. Spun rayon has short fibers which become fuzzy and tear as you pull, which is frustrating. Read the labels before you buy to be sure you are buying cotton yarns. Colorful all-cotton rug yarns, especially the lighter weight, are best. They are excellent for hardware-cloth stitching, heavy canvas, and burlap.

Stranded cotton is not satisfactory for children; the needle cannot be anchored, the strands pull unevenly, and large stitches produce a flat, uninspiring texture. Pearl cottons are good in sizes 3 and 5 (the lower the number, the heavier the yarn); size 3 is particularly suitable. These come in skeins, balls, or tubes.

Besides department stores, many excellent needlecraft stores carry a choice of good brands. Patronize those in your vicinity and encourage their growth. If there are no such stores where you live, you can order by mail from most stores. The Needlecraft Shop, 13561 Ventura Blvd., Sherman Oaks, Calif. 91403, has a large assortment of many brands. Lily Mills' light cotton rug yarn "Sugar and Cream," found in many stores, is frequently used in schools.

Wool yarns, such as those used in knitting, 3- or 4-ply, are suitable as soon as the child is old enough to handle them and avoid tangles. Persian and crewel yarns, which come in a wide variety of colors are also suitable. For young children, use single strands: double strands are apt to pull unevenly. Don't overlook variegated yarns; they can create exciting effects. Good wool yarns, and especially wool-and-nylon yarns, come in many beautiful colors on inexpensive small cards. Wool-and-nylon in a fine 3 ply is crisper than most all-wool yarns and is pleasant to use. Cards are useful when a small quantity of one color is needed.

String comes in many colors and types: soft, waxy, or rough like jute. Heavy yarns such as roving or rug filler are too heavy to pull through cloth but they can be useful couched with a thinner thread. The frame around the Teddy bear and the center of the tummy (see frontispiece) are Couched roving. Weavers often have fascinating left-over yarns. As children become older, encourage them to collect lengths of yarns, to experience variations in texture as well as color: thick and thin, shiny and dull, smooth and rough. Using cotton and wool yarns with linen, silk, and metallic threads gives a rich effect. Yarn collecting can be the basis of interesting studies in color and texture values, in blending and contrasting.

You will learn by experience what length of yarn is best for each child as this varies with the child. Start with approximately 28 inches, shorter for the very young. Too long a piece stretches the arm too far; it tends to tangle or fray. The child can learn to cut his own lengths, perhaps using the width of his table as a guide. He can also learn to make a knot, as described on page 19.

NEEDLES

Tapestry needles are best for children; they have a long eye, easy to thread, and are not too sharp. The size of the needle used depends on the age of the child (the smaller the hand, the larger the needle), on the weight of yarn chosen, and on the texture of the cloth. The needle should be slightly thicker than the yarn, in order to open a passage of sufficient size for the yarn to

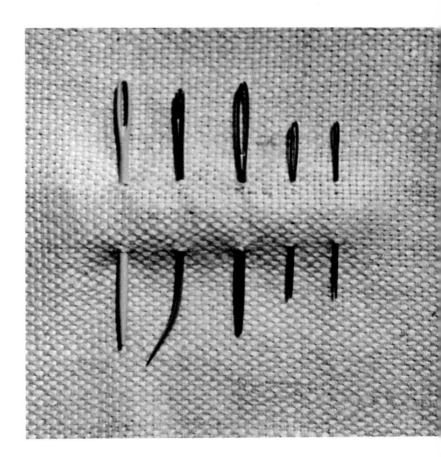

From left to right: plastic needle, curved needle, tapestry needle size 14, tapestry needle size 17, crewel needle size 1.

slide through without tugging. Sizes are marked by number, the higher the number, the finer the needle.

Use tapestry needles size 14 — sometimes called rug or yarn needles — for preschool children and for school-age beginners at almost all levels until they have achieved finger control. This happens fast around the third grade. Size 14 also comes with a sharp point under the name of chenille or couching needle for rugs.

There are plastic needles made in approximate size 14. These can be used for very young or for handicapped children. Whenever possible, however, use metal needles. Some plastic needles come with the eye bulging out. These are not suitable for drawing thread through fabric. Choose one with an eye such as pictured.

For most work by school age children, especially after the second grade, tapestry needles size 17 are good. Size 18 is often more easily available and can be used; it is a little harder to thread than size 17 and may mean tugging unless finer threads, such as pearl cotton size 5 or 3-ply wool, are used.

A long-eyed crewel or embroidery needle size No. 1 is good when a sharp pointed needle is necessary — for instance if the material is closely woven. Darning needles are long and thin; their use can be difficult.

Some needles used successfully by children are those with just the end curved, preferably the 3-inch length. They are called sack, bag, or candlewick needles (NOT the circular upholstery needle) and can be used only on loose weave materials such as burlap. This needle is particularly good for work in the center of large burlap pieces such as murals, where working the needle from back to front is difficult. These curved-end needles are wonderful for children and adults with various handicaps.

NEEDLE SUBSTITUTE

When a child is working on hardware cloth with squares $1/8$ inch or larger, a needle is not necessary if the tip of the yarn is suitably hardened. Spread and rub Elmer's glue on about $1^{1}/_{2}$ inch of one end of the yarn, twisting it into a point and letting it dry thoroughly on a piece of wax paper. Yarns should be prepared well ahead of time because cotton takes at least 15 minutes to dry; wool takes much longer and may have to be treated twice. Rayon does not absorb the glue well. Cotton is best for this.

This approach is particularly helpful for a child in bed, at home or in a hospital. It will keep him profitably occupied for long periods, using his hands with no danger of pricking himself and no risk of lost needles floating around. It is helpful for groups of children in institutions where needles might not be acceptable, for physically handicapped, blind, retarded, or disturbed children. It is possible, though not as satisfactory, to make a reasonable needle substitute for use on hardware cloth by wrapping the last inch of the yarn tightly with about an inch of masking or cellophane tape, cut at an angle and started with the point.

OTHER THINGS NEEDED

A strong shoe box at school (see page 21), a basket at home are useful to keep the odds and ends needed for stitchery.

Children should have a pair of good scissors. These should cut well and the ends should be rounded rather than pointed. Thread a yard of colorful ribbon through the two circles and tie the ends together. I do this to all my scissors; it makes them easy to find.

In addition to yarns, needles, and scissors, include two small pieces of soap, in a little plastic bag, for threading the needles, two pieces of dressmaker chalk, one light and one dark, and a thimble. A thimble for the middle finger of the right hand makes pushing a needle through much easier.

Other useful supplies would be a piece of nylon crinoline and a nylon-tip pen, a few sheets of strong layout paper, a sheet of dressmaker carbon, and a small box of pins to secure cut-out designs and couched threads in place. A few beads, interesting bits of braid, especially metallic, and scraps of colorful materials can be kept for added accents.

STITCHERY NOTEBOOK

As children's interest in stitchery grows, encourage them to keep a loose-leaf notebook in which they can paste clippings related to their work. Small samples of individual stitches with variations can be kept, sewn on to a sheet of paper. It is a good place for sketches and for noting ideas for future stitcheries. In it can be kept names and addresses of stores where supplies can be found; also names of books to be consulted, clippings from magazines, pictures which could be used as a source of inspiration.

Stitchery of imaginary flowers by Julie, age 8, made into a cushion by her mother.

FINISHING AND MOUNTING THE STITCHERY

With the stitchery placed right-side-down on a double thickness of wool blanket or soft towels, the back of the piece can be pressed gently with a steam iron.

If the stitchery is puckered, as often happens when children use burlap without a frame, it is usually possible to stretch it back into shape by the following method. First run masking tape, 1/4- to 3/8-inch width, behind the edges, if this was not done previously. On a piece of strong paper, tacked to a board (insulation board is best) or heavy cardboard, draw the outside lines of the material as they should be, squaring the corners. Over the drawn lines, lay a piece of transparent plastic as a barrier against stains from the board or cardboard; the squared outline should be visible. Lay the stitchery face down on the plastic (face up if the stitches are quite raised), and pin it in place with rustproof pins or thumbtacks, every half inch. Start at a top corner, pinning and stretching to keep to the line. If thumbtacks are used, they should not be pushed all the way in, otherwise they leave a circle on the material.

When the whole piece is pinned down, dampen it thoroughly, either with spray starch, which works well on burlap, or with a sponge or wadded towelling. If the material or threads are not color fast, be careful not to wet too much or the colors will run; even washable colored burlap is apt to run — that is one of the advantages of using natural or white. Ink that is not indelible is also apt to run. Let the piece dry thoroughly over night before taking out the pins. It is amazing how well a badly puckered piece can be straightened out.

Children love to see their pieces mounted and displayed. If the stitchery has been worked right to the edge, placing a mat on it makes it look important. If there is a free margin around it, turning the edges back over a piece

Some of Eleanor's early stitcheries were mounted at home on a board; the pieces were separated by brown grosgrain ribbon. After mounting, a flat piece of wood was attached across the top and a matching piece across the bottom.

of cardboard and holding them down with masking tape or staples is satisfactory; or a frame can be made, such as those described on page 162, and the material stretched over the edges and stapled on the back (see the back of picture, page 160). Narrow slats of balsa wood can be glued over the edges of the material and painted a suitable color. This is what James did around his stitchery, shown on page 50. Minor's bee was framed professionally, giving a boost to his ego. (See Color Page 30, C-9.) Kathy's caterpillar, Color Page 43, C-21, also framed professionally, was stretched and stapled on a piece of 1/4-inch-thick plywood and backed with poster board. Molding was used to make a 7- by 20-inch frame around the sampler of all the stitches described in this book.

I mounted Eleanor's first stitcheries by placing them on a board 25 by 14 inches, separating the four pieces with brown ribbon, and fastening a 3-inch-wide piece of flat wood, stained brown, over the top and bottom. Another way is to insert the top and bottom edge of the cloth between two thin slats of wood, the front piece stapled on from the back, the back piece screwed to the back of the front piece. If it is a wall hanging, the top can be hemmed wide enough for a wooden or brass rod to be inserted, or a casing can be made by sewing a tape on the back, wide enough for a rod. If the wall hanging is lined, leave an opening at both sides of the top and bottom to allow for inserting a curtain rod or dowel, which can extend a little at the ends and hang over hooks. Another way, for a light piece, is to use a heavy yarn and Blanket-Stitch the top edge to a rod. For a large piece, an effective way is to sew loops or doubled cloth or ribbon along the top and run the rod through, as was done on the children's banner, page 140. The rod can be painted to blend or contrast.

It is a challenge to think up ways of displaying stitcheries attractively to reward children for their effort.

Opposite: Sampler of all the stitches described in the book, in the same order, worked by the author.

Index of Stitches

*Try these first, if you don't know where to start.